# I Hope They're Right

*a memoir . . . sort of*

BY JONATHAN D FISHER

I Hope They're Right

Copyright © 2021 Jonathan Fisher. All rights reserved. No part of this book may be used or reproduced in any manner whatsoever without the written permission of the author.

Printed in the United States of America.

ISBN: 9798775938413

Self-published on Kindle Direct Publishing. For sale on www.amazon.com.

# ACKNOWLEDGEMENTS

This is the hardest part of the book for me. I wish I could remember and thank every person who ever believed in me. To those of you who have, thank you. To my family, I love you and appreciate you. To Steph, I don't think this book actually happens without you. To Niki, for sticking it out and for your expertise. To Jon, for forever having a place for me to turn. To Beth, for making my dream a reality when I felt like I needed the final push. To all of my readers for providing valuable feedback. To Kristina, for never allowing my confidence to waiver and believing I was capable of great things. To any person who has ever offered a kind word. To every character in this book for impacting my life for the better. To you, for picking this up and giving me a shot. Thank you.

**For everyone who told me that I could make something of myself. That I could change the world. This is for you.**

You have wonderful morals and values that make you the loving, determined person that you are! Jon, you have so much support from so many people who love you!

You have seriously made such a positive impact on my life Jon. I really and truly can say that I love you with all of my heart.

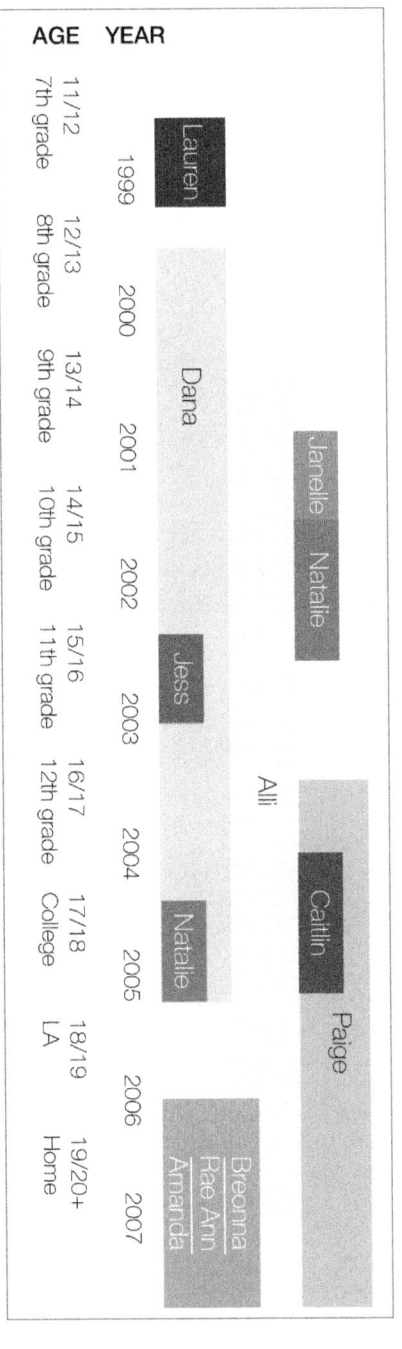

# PROLOGUE

In 2020, during a global pandemic, I walked into my storage unit looking for a piece of recording equipment that I thought I had lost. What I stumbled into was a vortex of memories and reminders of my formidable teenage years and the cast of characters who made me who I am today.

The mission of this book is to bring together multiple parts of my life to present a cohesive collection of stories, poems, songs, personal encounters, and my own take on them. With a "love life" that started at eleven years old and in seventh grade, I have a lot to share and to tell. Over twenty-five years, I've done my best to keep everything I can. I still have notes from girls, old phone numbers, letters, gifts, and the stories that go along with them.

I was around eight years old and in the fourth grade when I read a poem called "Casey At The Bat." This would lead me to write my first ever poem, about my brother Jeff, and would be the groundwork for a creative future. Since then, I've written hundreds of poems, songs, lyrics, notes, and more. I've had thousands of conversations, and I have countless memories of what it was like to go through those daunting years as an overly mature, emotionally active boy, trying to discover what it was that I was meant to do and who I was meant to be.

What I am certain of, proven by my recent discoveries, is that I had an army of supporters. People who believed in me beyond my wildest dreams and felt that I was going to make something of myself. That I was different, I was passionate, I had the "soul" to do it, and that no one was "like me." It's not that I haven't worked my ass off to try and make some of those dreams come true, and some even have. **But at times, it is hard to be convinced that I can do something that changes the world.**

**They all thought that I could, and *I hope they're right.***

# A LETTER TO THE READER

Dear Friend,

Thank you for being here with me. Thank you for picking up this book and deciding that this was a journey that you wanted to go on. Thank you for including me in your life, bringing me into your home, and sharing this time with me.

Though I do intend to tell you more about how I got to this point, I want to start with a small bit of backstory that I believe is necessary in order to read everything else in context. In the early part of 2012, I proposed to my girlfriend of four years and she said "yes." About one year later, I would be informed that this engagement was ending. We then embarked on six awful months of trying to reconcile our issues. We were not successful.

The relationship was unhealthy, and now years removed from those memories, I do realize how it was for the best. Though I saw some of the darkest times of my life in the months that followed, I fought hard to get that life back. But I wasn't going to settle for the status quo, I was given an opportunity at a rebirth and I took it.

However, I do not want to mince words. That relationship ending basically broke me. When I say they were dark times, I mean it. I wasn't sure I'd ever get back to "normal." I wasn't sure I'd ever figure it out again. What I know now, is that for almost five years of my life, I lost myself. I transformed into someone I never wanted to be and went to a place I never want to visit again. Since, I have found and continue to find myself daily. I could never have written this book ten years ago, but today I can.

In these pages, you are going to travel with me through

decades of my life. Reading some of my most personal experiences, insights, and triumphs. I couldn't have done this if it weren't for that relationship ending and deciding that life was too short to hold back. Everything that I've done since that experience has been a reminder that second chances do not always come, and when they do, we have a duty to take advantage.

To date, this book is my greatest accomplishment to rise from the ashes of those broken memories. I would not be anywhere near the person I am today without having experienced such a traumatic time.

It really does mean everything to know you're holding this piece of me. Let's begin.

With love,

*Jonathan D Fisher*

### JEFF

Jeff you're my brother, my idol, my charm
I can't disagree you have the best throwing arm
You stand on the mound, you wind up and throw
You throw about 90, you give them a show
The ball goes to the catcher's mitt, the ump says "Strike!"
You move up a little and say "Go take a hike!"

Then when you bat, you swing with all might
You swing so hard the ball goes out of sight
Over the fence, dead center field
You made them so scared they all got a shield
You run around the bases, then touch home plate
When you get older you'll be one of the greats

c. 1994

**TIME**

Why does time fly and where does it go
Why does time fly I wish I did know
Does it go through the window or even the door
Does it go through the crack on the very top floor
Does it go through the crannies or even the nooks
Is there such a thing as time flying crooks
There is one thought I wish I did know
Why does time fly and where does it go

c. 1995

# LAUREN

I'D LIKE TO ADDRESS SOMETHING EARLY ON. As you read, some of these dates and ages are going to seem odd. My birthday is on October 24. This put me in that small date range to potentially start school slightly early. I was actually at the very back of that range. However, I tested in and was in first grade at five years old. This set the stage for me to be a year younger than most of my peers at each grade level.

I'm not yet entirely sure how this affected my life and the way I lived it, especially when I was young. Academically, I think I fit in just fine. This seemed to make sense since I was learning the same things as everyone around me. What seems odd now and probably was odd then, is that I was very mature for my age, and even my grade. I was over-thinking before it was cool. I thought I was going to go to Harvard and would be the poet laureate of the United States. I read Robert Frost at eight and didn't think it to be slightly strange.

This doesn't mean I wasn't a typical boy who loved backyard baseball and tackle football. Took BMX bikes to the park and soaked in the sun. I think I was able to strike a balance. I believe what they call "emotional IQ" is what I possessed in a big way. I could assimilate easily, but not by necessity. I enjoyed the different versions of myself that I could access.

There is one thing for certain, I was girl-crazy at a young age. I can look back at these memories through the lens of a thirty-three-year-old who understands my intimacy with human connection. But I didn't know what it was at the time. I was emotional as hell, I was thoughtful, I was passionate and a bit abrasive, but I wanted to be good. So, I tried to be good.

I was eleven years old when seventh grade started. Thrust from elementary school into the lion's den where one hundred kids in my grade swiftly turned to five hundred or more. Kids from a dozen or so towns, different socio-economic backgrounds, all thrown together to figure it out. Again, I was eleven.

I was excited to learn, excited to have more teachers, to make new friends, to experience everything that I could. More than anything, I was truly excited to be surrounded by so many damn girls. And truth be told, when I look back, this was where it all really started.

A couple of months into seventh grade, I began to get the lay of the land. I was meeting people, making friends, and doing what kids do. A girl caught my eye, Lauren. She was bleach blonde, cute, and kind of a tomboy. Most of her friends were boys, but they all accepted me and it felt nice to belong.

Eventually, in the late fall of 1998, I asked Lauren if she would be my girlfriend. I genuinely don't have a great recollection of how that came to pass, but it did. Ultimately, we were a "couple." We would hang out and watch movies like *Armageddon*, go on haunted hayrides, and go bowling. Somehow, at that age, we actually managed to "date."

I come from a family that says "I love you" often. We say it when we get off of a phone call, when we leave one another's home, and in texts just as a reminder. I remember always wanting that with a girl, to say "love you" before saying goodbye. I did that with Lauren. I find it funny to look back and think of a twelve-year-old doing that. And she said it back. I was learning.

My age did show at times, however. Or at least my lack of female interaction. I could be shy at times, even scared. I had never kissed a girl before. I don't even mean a real kiss, I mean at all. But she had. The "real" kind.[1] I was in over my tiny, little head. I wanted to! I wanted to have that first kiss and experience what that connection felt like, but I was hesitant. I wanted it to have meaning and have it be an experience. Truthfully, she would kind of pick on me for not doing it sooner. This would be a bit of a theme for me.

However, as fate would have it, we were together one night at her house right before Christmas. She was walking me out to leave and in her front yard, with Christmas lights shimmering all over the house, we finally kissed. A hug and a small peck but it was everything to me. It was why I felt like I waited, it was why I felt like connection was important. My racing heart and the butterflies in my stomach. The tiny, intimate culmination of my wants and fears colliding. I see this all now and I can understand and process it, but I'm pretty sure I was clueless then. I was twelve.

---

[1] There's no cool or non-corny way to explain the difference between kisses. I got sick of writing "French" kiss because it drove me nuts to read it back and sound like I was a child. Moving forward, I'm using kiss and "real" kiss as differentiators. Trust me, we won't need this reference often.

## MY HOMEWORK FLEW OUT THE BUS WINDOW

My homework flew out the bus window,
it wasn't a sight to see.
For when I fail my English class,
grounded I will be.

I was sitting in seat twenty-five,
the last seat on the right.
And all of a sudden the wind blew it away,
with all its windy might.

I walked into the classroom,
without my head held high.
My teacher asked me where it was,
I replied, "It's in the sky."

So, when you do your homework,
don't do it on the bus.
'Cause if it flies out the bus window,
all your teachers start to fuss.

c. 1999

Jen,

Hey! What is UP NEMH? Anyway sorry it is taking me so long to decide if I want to go out w/ you or not. But see last year I really liked you and then after you were going out w/ Katie and Christina I just thought oh well he's going out w/ them. But then I liked you this year and when you asked me out I was suprised, but anyway (if any of that made sense) Yeah, I will go out with you. So I hope after we break up we can be friends. Well I gotta go? Cya!

always,
Kami

*I really appreciate that she wanted to be friends after we broke up, before we even started dating.*

```
KAMIE,

KAMIE YOUR MY GILFRIEND WHAT ELSE CAN I SAY,
YOU ARE GREAT IN EVERY SINGLE WAY,
YOU HAVE A SMILE THAT STRECHES FOR MILES, THAT CAN
LITE UP ALL THE SKY
I GUESS SINCE YOUR MY GIRLFRIEND, IM A VERY LUCKY GUY
I HOPE WERE TOGETHER FOR A LONG, LONG, TIME
I LIKE YOU SO VERY MUCH, IT COULD ALMOST BE A CRIME
EVERY TIME IM NEAR YOU, IM NEVER EVER SAD
EVERY TIME IM AWAY FROM YOU, IM EVEN SOMETIMES MAD
THERES NO OTHER WAY TO PUT THIS, THERES NOTHING
ELSE TO SAY
BUT YOUR ARE VERY BEAUTIFUL IN EACH AND EVERY WAY.


                                        LOVE,
                    JON


            HAPPY BIRTHDAY!!
```

*This poem was written in September of 1999. I wanted you to see the original font and the solid spelling/grammar.*

Jon~
Hey hun! What's up? N2MH! This class is so dumb. I always get yelled at. And yes I will go w/ you to the Christmas dance. Thanks for thinking of me. You are so sweet, I ♥ you. Well I dunno what to say so C ya! Oh yeah, thank you for asking me, b/c I thought you didn't like me anymore!

Call me!

♥ Kamri

Sorry short!

---

*I don't think we ever went to the dance together.*

# DANA

**HERE'S WHAT I THINK OF WHEN I THINK OF DANA.** It was a Friday night, we were at a high school football game, and we were in eighth grade. I kept hearing that this girl liked me, but I didn't know a ton about her. She was very sweet, and I thought she was insanely cute. Her friends kept asking me what I thought, and I remember balking. I remember waiting much of the evening, until we were all walking out the gates of the stadium to say to her friends, "Tell Dana I said yes."

And like that, we were twelve-year-olds dating. We would call each other on the phone and talk at school. I'm sure we exchanged plenty of notes, but there wasn't much else. I kind of remember trying to make plans with Dana and not much coming of that, I don't think we ever went on an actual date that year. But we were laying the groundwork for a real friendship.

I honestly don't think I ever stopped loving Dana from that point forward. We were staples in one another's lives. We shared a ton of similar friends, attended all of the same parties, and really grew together. There's this tendency to always say "I wish I knew then what I know now." I get it, it's kind of a neat sentiment, but it's bullshit, right? Growth is a necessity and experiences are what grow us.

In the late summer of 2000, as we were preparing for ninth grade, my band played a show at a park in Cranberry Township. I met a girl there, her name was Bridget. She was one grade ahead of me in school. That night, she asked me to the homecoming dance and I happily accepted. It felt really nice. This older, popular, and beautiful girl asking me? I was on top of the world.

Then, a month or two later, we went to homecoming. If there was ever a person who defied the phrase "dance with the one that brought you," it's me. And I'm not proud, but it's true. I spent much of that evening seeking out Dana. Mostly for the fast songs but even some slow songs, if I remember correctly, which went against high school dance protocol. We continued to have these emotions that neither one of us was all that good at containing.

There was an after party that night. Which, as I write this, sounds insane. But there was. And we all went. My date included. But I took this opportunity to spend time with Dana. At that point I had kind of ruined things with my date, and I had a real tendency to ride emotional waves in real time. Another theme.

I can picture the house and some of the people, but most of the details of the night escape me. Until it was time to leave. When I knew I'd be leaving for the night, I had my mind made up. I walked to the bottom of a staircase to find Dana once again; she was already coming down the stairs. I told her I was leaving, I gave her a hug, and without hesitation, I kissed her. Our first kiss.[2] It wouldn't become my modus operandi to just kiss a girl this way too often; it was usually quite the opposite. I think it's an interesting part of the juvenile side of my reminiscing.

Dana and I would begin dating for a second time after that. We attempted to find moments to be together or to see if we could last

---

2  It was a "real" kiss.

longer than a few weeks. We continued our talks on the phone, our note writing. We remained glorified friends. Some childish title put on what was really nothing more than two people beginning to see their connection. And the attempt failed, and we couldn't ultimately date for longer than a few weeks. The title was removed.

When I think back, I believe Dana was my first real crush. I had obviously "dated" prior and had crushes before, but she was the first girl to really burrow into my heart. We would say "Love you" by the time we were about thirteen years old. And sure, that's what silly kids do, and she wasn't the only girl I'd say that to, but she's the one to whom I'd say it from that point forward. "Luv ya" and "you too" would eventually become "I love you." We understood that much.

The friendship continued, and we'd both find ourselves interested in other people as time moved on. We'd both get the question every time, "Well, what about Dana" or "What about Jon?" That's what we were known as. How could someone possibly come in and penetrate this fortress of a partnership that we had built. But we weren't dating, and we had to figure it out.

Our friendship wasn't without difficult times. When emotions ran high, we were as susceptible as any young teenagers to petty squabbles. The below conversation is a great example:

---

**February 17, 2001**

**dAn▓▓24:** OK I have a Q I found these lyrics and I think its kinda how you feel about me but Im not sure
**dAn▓▓24:** look
**dAn▓▓24:** Unbelievable
You burden me with your questions
You'd have me tell no lies
You're always asking what it's all about
But don't listen to my replies
You say to me I don't talk enough

But when I do I'm a fool
These times I've spent, I've realized
I'm going to shoot through
And leave you

The things, you say
Your purple prose just gives you away
The things, you say
You're unbelievable

You burden me with your problems
By telling me more than mine
I'm always so concerned
With the way you say
You've always go to stop
To think of us being one
Is more than I ever know
But this time, I realize
I'm going to shoot through
And leave you

Seemingly lastless, don't mean
You can ask us
Pushing down the relative
Bringing out your higher self
Think of the fine times
Pushing down the better few
Instead of bringing out the clues
To what the world and everything anger to
Brace yourself with the grace of ease
I know this world ain't what it seems.

What the fuck was that
It's unbelievable

**J Dawg Fish:** Kind of, parts of it
**dAn▓▓24:** ok
**J Dawg Fish:** Well, i gotta klean my room for a little, oh ya guess what?
**dAn▓▓24:** what?
**J Dawg Fish:** I still love you! ttyl
**dAn▓▓24:** I love you more...cya hun

*I had to research these lyrics because I couldn't figure out the song. I now find it to be absolutely hilarious, though the message was actually clear. I also thought it was super cool to use a K almost anywhere a C belonged. Today, I know how to spell "clean."*

Ninth and tenth grade swirled with Alli, Mindy, Brittany, Janelle, and others. Eventually, Natalie would come into the picture in a big way, and that would set the stage for a hiatus. As I'm digging through all of the memories I have of Dana, the last thing I can really find before our "break" is a poem I wrote on November 29, 2001. There's more after the hiatus, but I would begin dating Natalie around Christmas of that year, so there's a clear blank spot in the relationship between Dana and I. Here's what I wrote:

*So many times I can sit here and type*
*So many times I can say*
*Thank you for all the things you've done*
*And always making my day*
*And so now I'll sit and write again*
*And say it another time*
*And just another poem I'll write*
*With Dana in every line*
*'Cause it sort of represents my life*
*All the poems I write*
*'Cause the pictures always run through my head*
*And they show Dana every night*
*Whether we're fighting, but mostly we're not*
*I'll always know you're there*
*And I hope you feel the same about me*
*'Cause I love you and I really do care*
*Now I just thought it was a good time*
*To say my thoughts again*
*'Cause most of the times I say your name*
*It ends with an Amen*
*'Cause I just can't thank this world enough*

*For giving me a friend like you*
*Someone who wasn't afraid to be herself*
*Someone who always stayed true*
*Yeah, we always have our fights*
*Go through easy and tough*
*But that's what makes a relationship work*
*Cause neither of us have bluffed*
*Never ever been false with each other*
*Always spoke our minds*
*And that's why I love you so much right now*
*And will till the end of time*
*True love shows when things are bad*
*And things are out of place*
*And every time I have a bad day*
*My thoughts always build your face*
*And show me there's someone out there*
*Someone that makes it worthwhile*
*And I know if I'm ever in a tough spot*
*All I have to do is dial*
*And when I look in the sky each night*
*And think of where you are*
*I look at every light that glows*
*And wish on Dana Starr*[3]

*Dana, I Love You*
                    *Love,*
                      *Jon*

---

[3] Dana's middle name is Starr. Which I always thought was so damn cool. So, I used it a lot.

I have multiple poems like this. I have instant messenger conversations and handwritten notes, as you've seen and will see. And they all seem to coincide with that timeline. I would be remiss not to mention that Dana and I did have tenth grade German class together and so we still had a friendship, it just wasn't as intense. It was in that class that Dana helped me develop my "autograph." I'll always remember that, and she would always make sure I did.[4]

Natalie and I dated from December of 2001 until early 2003. I'll detail this later. Early 2003 was eleventh grade, and Dana and I happened to have another German class together that year. After a summer spent almost entirely with Natalie, this class would once again bring Dana and I back together to some degree. After Natalie and I broke up, I turned to Dana in a big way.

Around all of these years, Dana was dating. It was kind of odd sometimes because they were friends we both shared, but that's high school. Eventually, she would begin dating her true "high school sweetheart." They would be on and off at times, I would be sort of single at times, and again, things never really lined back up.

This writing has been emotional. This stroll down "Dana Lane" has genuinely hit me like a ton of bricks. I've cried on multiple occasions and found myself struggling to eat. All of this isn't just some silly project, this all means an immense amount to me. I say this because I'm re-reading everything, and I know I haven't even gotten to the emotional parts. That's where it all comes back together for me.

Our senior year, Dana and I remained close and continued to root one another on. Doing the best we could to support each other through tough times, relationships, and anything else that came our

---

[4] I need to apologize to Frau Sibeto for how much time Dana and I really did spend during her class working on my autograph for when I was "famous."

way. We celebrated the ending of our high school days, we swore we'd always be in each other's lives.

The summer of 2004 came and went and suddenly we were all off to college. At that time, it seemed like we were all destined to grow apart, and I think that's natural. Dana and I remained in contact through instant messages and did our best to keep each other updated. She and her boyfriend went to the same college together; that was the progression. But then something happened.

On March 7 of 2005, towards the end of my time in college, Dana had a spring break. While home on her break, she decided that she was going to come visit me at school. This seemed like a big deal, like validation that our friendship was still strong, and we would persist. I blew everything off that day and nervously waited for Dana to arrive.

When she got there, I proudly introduced her to all of my friends and then we went to my room to talk and be together once again. It was surreal. It was gut wrenching. It was incredible. We laid there for hours simply talking and watching TV and smiling. Did I mention Dana's smile? Oh man. Incredible. She had this big, wide smile with amazing teeth and two adorable dimples. It was a real soft spot for me.

What this did, however, was what we both likely feared but chose to ignore. It reignited a spark. The comfort, the familiarity, the love. That honest love. It reminded me what love felt like and reminded us both how easy it was. There was no kiss, only contentment. She left that night, and my stomach was in knots. I eventually did what I always do, I wrote.

**March 14, 2005**

Ms. Dana Starr.

 Well it's currently about 4:30 in the morning and I find myself here doing the one thing I do well and unfortunately the thing to which you often fall victim, writing. This is quite a peculiar verse for me to write however because I've rarely been in the position to say the things that will be said in the proceeding lines.

 Too many things have been said and done and once again you and I find ourselves in the midst of an emotional fist fight. Whether it be against each other or our own selves, the pain is surely real. I find myself also enjoying the intro to this essay much more than I'm going to enjoy the brunt of it, hence the stalling but to fight tears something must be done. Speaking of, I received a text message via cell phone from you tonight that read "why do I still miss you?" And while I feel I have all the answers to your conundrum, that's not the reason for my writing.

 That message broke me into pieces. I was sitting down with eight of my closest friends to play cards and had to look away and keep tears from running down my face. I had to hide the swelling of my eyes and can only thank God they didn't have to see my heart because an ambulance was more than likely nowhere to be found. Is this a guilt trip? No. Is it my last chance for peace with not only you but myself? Yes, because to be quite honest, I have to get this out. Oddly enough it's not like many previous feelings I've had, this one just doesn't hurt so bad but for some reason it means the most. Please prepare yourself for this writing to be lengthy, wordy, intense, and heartfelt. Not to mention loving, healing and psychologically cleansing. So let's get started.

 You left here Monday night and without saying a word we both knew we had the same thing on our minds. We love talking about our problems too much however to leave it at that. I had a catch on my end though, I knew you had a boyfriend, but did you know that? I could have sworn for a second there you may have forgotten; more so, made a distinct attempt to do so. But this could just be me and my stupid philosophies.

I walked back from the parking lot to a dorm room full of friends who were just ready to hound me with questions. Here was my favorite... "Why aren't you two dating?" Crying yet? Because I sure am. But do you want to know what I answered? Sorry, I'll tell you anyway. "I don't know." Now, it could have been an array of excuses such as a boyfriend, or California, or College, but those just weren't enough for me to justify letting you walk in and out of my life so often without taking a stab at something that felt so necessary. I had to look them straight in the eyes and say "guys, you don't understand, she's like the girl of my dreams but we've yet to find what the hell we're here for."

I prayed for you to get home and miss me. As much as I'd love to say I regret that, I don't. I almost even felt stupid at one point thinking I missed you this much and you could have cared less, but you did care. You told me numerous times that you're unaware as to why you miss me, but you do. That was the most devastating and beautiful thing I could have wanted to hear. But why do we miss each other so much? Why do we click so damn well when we're together? Why do I want to be the perfect guy when I'm around you and want everyone else to be jealous of what we have? Why when I think of the girl that fits perfectly with me, do I see you?

I'm probably pretty sure I have no idea what the answers are to these questions, but I've got a hunch. I had a conversation tonight *with my buddy Shane about the messages I've been getting from you and here is exactly what I said. "But Shane, she's the one girl that I could be away from for months, I could go to California while dating her, go to school while dating her, not give a shit what happened when we were apart because when I was with her, she'd be mine. And it is those times that make the time apart not matter." You know me, you know I don't have the personality to handle girls that freely, but with you, I do, for the reason I just explained. Because I truly only live each day the way it's supposed to be lived and if it's a day with you, then that's just a better day, and that's it.*

*I've surely changed over the last couple years when we weren't the closest of friends. I've learned a lot about myself and have learned to love the person I am. As miserable as I may be or seem, I've truly never been happier.*

*When we're together there's a lot of emotion. There's a past that's seemingly been left incomplete. A present that might be more confusing than the past, and a feeling that neither of us can understand but we know we like it. I might be going nowhere with this entire letter but it seems to be making me feel better so I'm sorry if you're just bored.*

*When we were younger Dana, we were younger. Four years later, we've cheated ourselves out of knowing a damn thing about the ability we have. I'd go so far as to call it a talent. We're content, so damn content with each other. You know what I love about that, I brag about that contentment, I brag about you. Almost as to say watch, watch this girl and I lie in this bed for a whole day, and whether something is said or not, whether we kiss or not, watch how happy both of us are when it's all done. I can only speak for myself but I've never experienced that and have never had a better feeling.*

*I honestly remember lying in that bed at about 5 o'clock already thinking God, I can't believe she already has to leave in seven hours. I skipped musical because that three hours with you meant more than anything deemed important at the time. I couldn't wait till you got here and I was able to introduce you to all of my new friends and show them what I've been bragging about for all this time. I never really did that in front of them before, and they read it like a book. They knew exactly why I felt the way I did and why I said the things I said. It was all about you.*

*Here's why this letter is very different from all the others. I'm not mad, I'm mildly upset and mildly confused but more than anything I find myself here wondering if this is worth a fight. Because I've never had to do that before. I've never had to completely stop somebody and say look! How are you not seeing what I'm seeing? To me the whole thing is so apparent it's bothersome but I unfortunately (or fortunately) have the side of being completely and utterly single.*

*You and I have always had what it takes but never had the maturity to handle what we knew. Now we do, and now it becomes harder than ever to think that maybe, just maybe we've not let ourselves see what we've always been supposed to see. Maybe it was too easy to just say we're no good for each other, maybe we were so scared that's all we could find to cover it up. Now after all this time though and finally spending some time with you it's hard to turn back years of believing one thing to believing another, but I think I've done it.*

*I think I've stopped believing that we just didn't work or that we just don't belong. Some things maybe just aren't that easy. I know what this all boils down to, believe me I do and I don't blame you one bit for turning your back to me completely (not that that's what you've done). The one thing I'm sick of doing though is rolling over every time something is in front of me that just isn't right at the time. That's pointless. I've done that probably one too many times and I'm pretty sure it's not been the best thing to do.*

*I've been completely true to myself this time and have been completely true to you. This is not a plea to get you, believe me it's not. I'm not here trying to ruffle your feathers just to see if this whole thing can work. I don't want to disturb the picture perfect life you have and I know I would give up anything to see you happy, if this is what it takes, so be it. I just didn't want to let another second pass without us getting to the core of our confusion.*

*Why do we miss each other Dana? I'd say it's a rhetorical question, because we both know. We both have always known and have yet to find a solution to the so called problem of missing each other. Maybe we deserve each other, maybe we don't but we can't make excuses anymore. We have to take this head on and deal with it because California is calling.*

*Love you, Jon.*

If I recall correctly, and I don't blame her, this letter wasn't received well. Mostly because I was sort of pouring it all out, and what sort of position did that put her in? She had a boyfriend; she had her life at school. She came to see me, and I had my chance to make a move or speak up, and I didn't. I cowered. I chose the moment over the big picture, story of my life. And she had to hear a week later from me about this instead of me manning up enough to say what I really wanted. I don't think I understood the extent of my love or how it was meant to be directed.

What this did do was really rekindle our relationship. Though it was going to be as friends, I was happy just to have had that day and to know that I still had my friend. The craziness wasn't over, we both liked communicating feelings to one another, even if it was at the worst times imaginable. I actually, just yesterday, brought this up to my closest friend. He said, "Really thought you'd end up with Dana at some point."

So, Dana and I continued to communicate, we got through the end of the school year, and I was preparing for my move to Los Angeles. We hung out a couple of times but what I remember best is my going away party. Like I said previously, my college friends had all met her and knew a bit of our history, and they kind of gave me that wink-wink-nudge-nudge when she arrived. I was excited that she made the time to be there, and that we were strong.

Other than those of my friends who were staying that night, Dana was the last to leave. My family owned a bar and restaurant, and that's where the party was. At the front of the building was a window that looked out onto Main Street. I walked Dana to her car as she was leaving, and all of the friends that were left piled around the window to see. We talked for a minute; I'm sure we were very emotional. Then we hugged for a very long time. This was love. Six years of love.

I walked back inside sort of smiling at everyone and they gave me some shit for not having kissed her. Again, the nuance was impossible to understand outside of Dana and I. It's like we had this secret, and no one else was going to be let in on it. We knew why things happened the way they did, but to the untrained eye, it probably looked like idiocy.

The next day I was set to leave for LA; Dana was there. She came to my house to help me finalize my packing and to see me off. Dana was the last person besides my family that I said goodbye to. She was there. She always was. She had a letter.

Jon,
Well this day is truly bittersweet. Sweet because I am so proud that you are going out there doing what you love, despite the odds, b/c you believe in yourself (as do I). Bitter because this very well could be the last time I see you (even though I hope it's not. I can't deny the reality of the situation). I've been thinking a lot about how our goodbye will go and every time I envision it, it is different ~~everything~~, however, it always ends with this weird anticipation that for some reason brings butterflies to my stomach. I'm so confused sometimes about our situation but despite the confusion I know that we will always be there for each other even if we are "worlds apart." Timing has never been our thing but this is your time and I pray that you will succeed beyond your wildest dreams even if you leaving brings a lump to my throat. I have so much faith in you but even more I have hope that you will learn and accomplish so much by taking this risk.

Regardless of how much I'm going to miss you I'm so proud of you. Thanks so much for all that you have done for me. Through the years I've known you as a crush, a boyfriend, and at times someone I didn't even talk to but through all those titles and feelings our friendship has remained true. There are few ppl that have been what you have been for me. Thanks so much for that.

So take this as the first letter you recieve from me while apart. I wish you all the best of luck and of course sunray's and Saturdays & perfect STARRY nights. I love you Jonathan.   Love, Dana

I found this letter five days ago from the time I'm writing this. I bet I've read it a dozen times. I've yet to read it and not cry; Dana loved me. She said the right things and she said honest things. She showed me the vulnerability I always asked of others. She said exactly what I needed to hear the day I was leaving. She validated all of the feelings I had and shared in the confusion. Dana and I had a couple of "our songs" through the years, but there was one we always came back to.

A friend of mine on a chorus trip in ninth grade showed me an acoustic CD of the band Vertical Horizon, *Running On Ice*. I remember having it in my discman and getting to track eleven. The song is called "Sunrays and Saturdays." *See Dana's note. On a bus full of my peers, I broke down immediately when I heard it for the first time. I knew this was the song Dana and I deserved, and I couldn't have ever said anything better to her, nor could I today. Stop now, listen to the song. Please.

> Always trying to make love out of care. The perfect recipe, but something wasn't there.
>
> It's not that we're bad together. We're just better off apart.
>
> Always trying to have one and one make two. And even though it never worked, I still feel love for you.
>
> And I wish you Sunrays and Saturdays and perfect starry nights. Sweet dreams and moonbeams and a love that's warm and bright. Sunrays and Saturdays and friendships strong and true. Oceans of blue and a room with a view to live the life you choose.

I've listened to this song at least eight times in the last three days. It brings me back to the moment I heard it, the moment I shared it with Dana, and each ensuing moment where we affectionately offered the other "Sunrays and Saturdays and perfect starry nights." There are songs that get me, but I truly believe that to this day, no one song more than this.

So, the letter. We stood outside at the bottom of my steps and I leaned against the wall. Dana and I, the final hours. The final minutes. Five years after "Tell Dana I said yes." Four years after our first kiss. Three months after lying in bed together all day. The letter said it all, and we both knew this was likely it. We hung on to that moment for as long as we possibly could. And I'm glad we did. I hope I have that moment forever.

Dana would go on to send me a birthday card, a Christmas card, and we would do our best to keep in touch. Me, struggling to figure out life as a nineteen-year-old artist in LA and Dana, going to school and focusing on her relationship. It's amazing how these things work. I remember so many of these details and so much about what we had, but I can't remember when we lost it. It's not all that identifiable. People erupt into your life and then, against your very will, they fade away.

Eventually, life takes over. Unless my memory serves me incorrectly, Dana and I really didn't see each other after that day except for coincidentally. Once at a friend's wedding and another at our high school reunion. I find that to be astonishing and a true heartbreak in life.

Dana went on to marry her high school sweetheart and I believe they have two boys. I see her brother now and again; I truly loved her whole family and they brought me in like I was one of theirs. It's now been about five years since that high school reunion, and we haven't spoken since yesterday when I knew I was going to write this and just wanted to wish her well.

I hope that Dana has a similar memory of our past, and that I've done us justice. I hope that she cherishes the parts we played in each other's lives and the room and love we gave one another to grow. Still today, even from afar, her happiness makes me a happier person.

Dana, thank you for your love. When you could have placed it anywhere, you placed it on me. You taught me more than I could have ever wished. Thank you for believing in me and allowing me to grow alongside you. Until I can no longer say it, I truly wish you Sunrays and Saturdays and perfect starry nights. I love you.

Dana and me during a chorus trip in 2002.

Jon,
Hey hun! How are you? I'm good. Sorry I couldn't get back online last night, my mom and I went shopping again and I thought we would be back at 8:00 but we didn't get back untill like 10:00. Bart said you called but by the time he told me it was late and I didn't wanna call to late. When I got home from the mall I checked my mail and I got your e-mail. Sorry I couldn't write back but I had to go to bed. I promise I will write back as soon as I get home from school today. Do you have to stay after again? Anyway, my mom said that I could see Scream 3 with you on Fri. so hopefully you and Seth are ok again. Ashley really likes Tyler, do you have any idea who he likes? Well write back if ya can cause I gotta let cha go now. I'm in homeroom and the bells gonna ring. Talk to ya later. Luv always,
*Meghan*

*Likely late 1999. I don't remember who Tyler liked.*

Jon,

Hey babe! How are you? I'm in bed right now and I just got your email. I feel so bad about my brother makeing fun of you. As soon as I read that I got so mad and yelled at him. I told him he was just jealous that he could never write a poem like that. I was looking through my pictures and I found my album from the Christmas Dance!! There is this picture I found, it is you and like Becca, Kim S, Ben V and some others. I cut them out so now I have a pic of you! It's right on the top of my computer so everytime I'm on (which is alot) I think of you. Also I have Barts yearbook open to page 29 so I can see your pic right before I go to bed everynight! ☺ I am also very excited about Friday. Sat. afternoon I'm leaving for my dad's b-day party. I will be home Sun. afternoon or Sun. night. Sorry bout not wearing a skirt today. I wanted to wear this one but it was at the dry cleaners so I couldn't. I have to wear one tomorrow (4 performing arts) so I will. Well I'm outa room so I have to let cha go! W/B Luv ya lots, meghan

*My big takeaway here... how I ever thought I was in the same league as someone who had their clothes dry cleaned in the eighth grade.*

## LIVING NIGHTMARE

Drifting into a depth
Understanding no return
When you can't cross back
Over the bridges you have burned
The meaning lost in wilderness
Of visions all serene
And you just keep slipping further
But don't know what it means
When the trail has been paved over
And your swimming path's been filled
And your future shattered from your past
And your dreams have all been killed
When your last string just slipped off
And your threads are going weak
And your wild imagination snaps at night
When you can't sleep
So don't go look to me
When I can't look to you
When things are all going for you
I'm the friend you never knew
So learn your lesson now
The chance can still become
But don't come cry to me right now
'Cause now I'm not the one

c. 2001

# ALLI

**BUCKLE. UP.**

The inspiration here is real; it was real. And boy did it last for a long, long time.

I met Alli in ninth grade. I was about thirteen. She had lived in our school district earlier in her life, moved down south, and was now back. I didn't know her before the move back, but I sure wanted to now. Alli was pretty, organically and genuinely pretty. But what truly made Alli the apple of my eye, was her heart. At an age when people sometimes forget how to treat one another, Alli was good.

Much to the theme of my high school days, I felt like Alli was a bit out of my league. I never believed I didn't have a lot to offer a girl, but I had a genuinely difficult time at that age being thrown into, and dating, a completely different socio-economic group. I didn't know what it was like to have money, and that was just my reality. Six of us lived in the two-story apartment above the bar my parents owned. I wouldn't change it for anything but it still took me some time to understand the differences between us. When I went to some of these girls' houses they were huge, perfectly clean. Parents would be cooking or baking or just hanging out. They'd come to my house, and it was a mess, lived in by four kids. My parents would be downstairs in the bar working at all hours. It was simply different.

However, I still only wanted to go after the best, and Alli was one of them. Throughout the madness of these early years in high school, we became close friends. It was never much of a secret who my crushes were. Firstly, I was fairly obvious, but secondly because it was always going to be the girls that everybody else was chasing as well. I believe most guys, when we were that age, weren't nearly as interested in dating as I was, and most were not mature enough to go through with it.

As Alli and I grew closer, I finally made my move. And in rather typical fashion, I wrote this poem on March 13 of 2001:

*I've known you for a year*
*But it seems much longer*
*'Cause every day you mean more*
*And my feelings grow stronger*
*My heart grows bigger*
*And fills with you*
*Giving me the strength*
*To want to pull through*
*Through the tough times*
*That we all sometimes meet*
*But you are the one*
*To pick me up off my feet*
*The one to bring me cheer*
*And brighten my day*
*Making me happy*
*In your adorable way*
*And I'm also here for you*
*As you are for me*
*To be the best to you*

*That I can be*
*So thank you for all*
*That you have done*
*You're such an amazing girl*
*And I know you're the one*
*And my feelings are strong*
*And I have no doubt*
*So I'll ask you right now*
*Do u wanna go out?*

It's amazing how much writing would be involved in this relationship. How this first poem would spark work that myself, and even some others, will remember for the rest of our lives.

Alli was pretty innocent. She was the kind of girl I didn't want to swear around, and someone who I wanted to be better for. I think this made me work even harder to prove to her the kind of guy I could be and the kind of guy she deserved to have. My real intention, always, is to make sure that I raise the bar for any guy that might come after. I definitely feel that way today, but I think it started at a pretty young age. I wasn't close to perfect, but I knew I wanted to be the chivalrous and kind male presence that I saw in the movies.

By this time in our lives, most of my friends, or those in our circle, had experienced our first real kiss.[5] Alli had not. This overwhelmed me for some reason. When that would likely feel like the perfect time to swoop in and be her first, I saw it in a totally different light. I didn't want to take away any of that innocence that she had. Even something as simple as a kiss.

We went through the basic motions. I would walk Alli to her bus each day after school and kiss her goodbye, but that was the extent

---
5  Again, note "real."

of that.[6] Honestly, I felt like the king of the school when I got to do that. And I wanted to make absolutely sure that I didn't squander the opportunity to be respectful and sincere with this wonderful girl. Also, I'll add, we didn't get many chances to be together outside of school. So, even if I did think there was going to be a good moment for it, I wasn't sure it would ever arise. And I sure wasn't going to do it at the front of our school on the way to her bus.

Then came Easter of 2001. The plan was to go to Alli's house, dye Easter eggs, and watch movies. This was kind of an assumed "date." This was when it was meant to happen. We started dating on March 13. Easter of 2001 was on April 15, also Alli's birthday. A month seemed like the appropriate amount of time, we were finally going to be one-on-one, and we'd finally be able to spend real time together away from school.

I still remember the inside of Alli's house. I remember dying eggs with her mom and her sister in the kitchen and having a blast. I remember Alli and I going into the living room right next door and lying on the couch together. We put on a movie, my arm around her, and my mind went nuts. I kept looking over at her, smiling. All of these adorable little fourteen-year-old moments. But nothing. I couldn't do it. And I never did.

Alli would later tell me that she wanted me to be her first kiss on that day. My brain just had other plans. I look back at this and I'm not overly surprised that I didn't do it. I mean, I'm the guy who still stops a girl before sex and asks if it's okay. And though she would have said the kiss was okay, I didn't find it to be as important as being a good boyfriend, being respectful, and being kind. She may have thought she was ready, but for some reason I couldn't draw that same conclusion. Not for her first "real" kiss.

---

6   Peck on the lips. It's all seeming very silly, right? Me too.

From what I can gather, Alli and I dated for about two to three months. So, even for the month or two that followed Easter, that kiss never came to be. But we would grow closer and build a friendship that would eventually take over for our relationship. During our sophomore and junior years of high school, Alli and I would grow apart somewhat. She had a couple of very close friends that I would eventually develop a thing for, and also, my future relationship with Natalie would pull me away from many of my friends.

Senior year, Alli would become our Homecoming Queen. This was no surprise to me, and not likely to anyone else in the school, especially considering how many of us voted for her. It's interesting the way things play out because it was also senior year that I would become class president for the second time. Alli and I stood at the forefront of our class. I like to think my classmates and I helped build each other to those points.

Later in our senior year, Alli and I would end up in a play together. I remember her sitting by herself in the auditorium during a rehearsal, and I walked over to talk to her. It was almost like the first time again. We had gone somewhat separate ways, and I hated that; I really did. That day, we got put back on track. We talked for a while and eventually when rehearsal was over, I offered Alli a ride to her car. We were rebuilding our friendship, and I felt like a piece that was missing had finally been put back into place.

Alli was destined for big things. She was a dreamer and when she dreamt it, she did it. Senior year ended, college came, and Alli and I didn't stay in touch all that often. Alli did come to my going away party in June of 2005, and I think after a year of not seeing one another, it was easy for us to find comfort in the other. That would start the next chapter of us staying in touch and rebuilding once again.

As you've heard and will continue to hear, that time after I moved was insane. There were emotions everywhere, I was trying to figure out a brand-new life, things were absolutely chaotic. Alli and I would talk now and again and do our best to keep in touch. Eventually, things would settle down, and I'd have a chance to reign my mind back in and begin a real process of moving on from anything that I could.

It had been quite some time since I had put into writing what Alli meant to me. I was in Los Angeles to create music and to hone my craft. So, on December 6 of 2005, I took a stab at writing her a song.

### WIN/WINN

*This will come out quickly*
*There's no time*
*For holding back the words that are falling off*
*The tip of my tongue*
*This is coming out easy*
*Easier than anything I thought I should have said*
*You are*
*From my point of view*
*Everything that's great about*
*Being alive*

*I don't want to call it perfection*
*But I have to admit that it's closer than anything I've seen*

*If the rest of your life continues*
*And nobody mentions a word*
*About the character you hold*
*The person you are*

*That's absurd*
*So I try and take mention, say thank you*
*No attempt at being profound*
*For the person you were, the person you are*
*And the person you will be*
*The next time around*

*It's getting much harder*
*I'm struggling to speak*
*I start to lose air*
*I start not to care*
*And my lungs begin to get weak*
*I'll start getting nervous*
*I'll start to turn red*
*To break up what I'm saying*
*From my lungs to my head*

*Where would we be*
*I mean, where would I be*
*If I couldn't say the things that I want to say*
*To a melody*

I would come to name this song "Win/Winn," a true homage to Alli. Ten days later, I wrote a letter that I wanted to give to Alli for Christmas. A few weeks after that, when I was back home visiting, I drove to Alli's, I played her the song, and I gave her this letter.

**December 16, 2005**

*Allison Blair ~*
*I don't know how to start this, I really don't. You're probably worried about where it's going but don't be, it's basically a*

*continuation of the card. Most cards fail to be as lengthy as I prefer so I'm stuck with the task of matching its grace.*

*For some reason this Christmas was all about letters to people. I pretty much wrote a letter to each of my family members. I just think more than anything else it allows me to really get my point across. This isn't my stab at being profound or seeing how well I can write. Nor is it some desperate plea for recognition or response. This is simply for you to understand the kind of person you are through my eyes.*

*I don't know why it took us the better part of six months to really start talking and getting our friendship back, but it did. You say everything happens for a reason, so maybe the time was to show me how to work through the weeds and find the flowers. Whatever the case, I'm beyond elated to have a friend like you in my life.*

*I can't ask you to understand how I really feel, but a lot of times it's a rough equivalent to lonely. It makes me a stronger person so the last thing you should do is feel sorry for me. I chose my life. The reason I mention that is because in this simple, partially lonely life I lead is a glimpse of optimism. She calls herself Allison. You really brighten my day beyond words. You have this glass is half full approach to everything and I adore it. Furthermore, I envy it and maybe I'm just crossing my fingers hoping if I get close enough a little can rub off.*

*If this letter had a thesis statement I guess it would be along the lines of you really make me want to be a different, better person. You know how to be strong; you know how to accomplish things without compromising any of your admirable convictions. More importantly, you can lean on others, and that may be the strongest thing of all.*

*We're somehow a lot alike. Everything you say I understand and vice versa which, coming from my whacked out mind, is quite rare.*

*But somehow it seems to compliment one another nicely. I really don't know what I'm trying to accomplish by writing this except maybe trying to let you know what an incredible person you are.*

*You're such a kind person with such a big heart and you manage to see the world in a light that nobody else can possibly see it in. You carry that light with you and people notice it and that's why they are just immediately attracted to you. I know you don't so much like thinking these things about yourself but you really need to always remember it.*

*There is so much about you that is so amazing. I'm only writing a letter so I can't put it all in here, had it been a novel, I had a chance. Just always keep in mind that you're an incredible girl with more than a lot to offer. Any person should be lucky to have you in their life, I know I am. You've made me feel so great about some of the things I've accomplished and it really isn't necessary but I really appreciate it. When things look down you manage to bring them right back up.*

*Ultimately, I just want to say thank you. Thank you for being yourself and being an incredible friend. You're an amazing person. I'm sure you know that. If at any point during your life others fail to realize that and recognize you as such, I can only hope that this tiny gesture can keep you reminded. I also hope that it can offer you at least a mere fraction of the gratification you deserve from the appreciation I have of you as a person. Thank you.*

Love Always,<br>Jonathan David Fisher

The letter simply reiterated what the song was meant to say. I always thought so highly of Alli, and I wanted to make sure she knew. But that's all it was, a quick visit home for the holidays and then back to LA. She loved the song and the letter and we became stronger. Ultimately, that song would make it onto my second album.

I came home for good in June of 2006. You'll read what the next nine months would look like. Dating, recording, song writing. In April of 2007, and I'm honestly not sure how we got to that point, Alli and I decided to go to a movie. I was completely under the assumption that it was as friends. We saw *Disturbia*. Alli has always been a physical person. She loved hugs, holding hands, standing close, cuddling, and the like. So, during the movie, when things would get intense, she would grab my arm and hold tight. I liked it, but didn't think much of it.

We would start hanging out a bit more after that. We'd do more together, and eventually we would both come to realize that we were developing some kind of feelings. I remember this time rather vividly. I remember thinking that after all these years and as highly as I regarded Alli, it seemed so bizarre. I felt in over my head; I felt like a lot of emotion was going to go into this simply based on our history as friends and crushes. I was elated, I really was. I was, what I would call, cautiously optimistic.

Six years after being those two kids sitting on a couch on Easter Sunday wondering if we would ever kiss, on May 4 of 2007, we finally did. I wasn't meant to be her first, but I was meant to be one. And when it happened, it felt like six years in the making. It was explosive. And on May 7, I sent Alli a letter.

*Allison,*

*I wasn't quite sure it was possible but you are seemingly as inquisitive as I am. That's not a bad thing, I quite like it, we're just that type of personality as it were.*

*I guess the first thing is that I just can't get you out of my head, and for that reason I felt the need to write this. I'm consistently all over the place; my mind wanders at rapid speeds. I also want to add that I've always adored you, so though presently it seems as if this letter was a bit premature, as far as I'm concerned, it's long overdue. There's a lot that I want to say and I'm sure it will be aggressive and overbearing, for which I apologize. I may also leave out a lot so if I remember it I'll cover it later. : )*

*It sounds silly that I would say to you that I feel you are out of my league. As I put it the other night, "not at your level." I'm a confident person; I believe in myself and am completely content with all of the things I encompass. I also have lived a life that is thus far, regret free. I very much live, and unfortunately at times, I very much learn. I guess I just always felt like I would never be the right guy for you. We come from pretty different places and hold amazingly different views. However, I think one thing that will always keep us close is the size of our hearts. You may show yours a bit better than I do and more people may take notice, but when I want, I can be a caring and kind person. I'm glad you recognize that, it means a lot. I've had a lot of recent run-ins with the situation we are presently in, unfortunately, the bulk of which have ended badly. I see things very differently than most people, nothing to me is simple. Everything is a puzzle to me, a puzzle which is in dire need of my attention and my solving. This is the reason I didn't want to let myself actually like you. I figured if we could play the friend card until you left, there would be no confusion and nothing to worry about. It obviously didn't work out as such. I'm not complaining, believe me. I just know myself well enough to know the consequences of a kiss, especially one with the one person in my life who I hold on a pedestal above all others. You may never comprehend what is seen when my eyes see* you. I wish someday you will, because everyone deserves at least one glance at something so wonderful.

So let me get to the point, which is the position we find ourselves in today. I wouldn't write this if I didn't feel it would speak volumes above anything else I could say to you via text. Hopefully it will help you as much as it is helping me. Since you asked me how I felt, I figured I'd give you the real version, rather than the abbreviated three sentences I sent on my LG.

When I start something with a girl, one I know I like, it immediately affects me. The reason for this is mostly because I'm not one for games. I used to be, but I found it to be a bit shallow and a bit dissatisfying. I have found that I might as well lay it all out there, and if it is received well or poorly, I can at least say I gave it everything I had, and nothing less. I don't like to hold back just because you might think I'm too intense, this is me, like it or not, it's real. I've become content with the idea that this is me. I really hope you like it, but if not, there's nothing I can do. Hence the reason I now wear my heart on my sleeve. If we both put it all out there, there's no questions and we both understand things much better.

So now that we've had these conversations as of late regarding where this is headed, I figured I'd throw all of this at you and let you do with it what you may. I have no patience, everything in my life is moving at sonic speeds. So in my honest opinion, if I could have it my way right now, here's how things would be. You and I would make a decision to be exclusive. I'm not saying the kind of relationship where everything is a hassle or needs an explanation. I'm just saying the peace of mind to know that at this moment in time, there's no one else but each other. I know that in one week's time my mind could completely change about the whole thing, I'm well aware yours could also. That's just life. We would never truly figure things out if we never give it a solid try.

I know you're moving and I know there's a lot involved with all of that but why not attack that obstacle when it's necessary rather than eliminating what could be a month's worth of happiness? Why not just dive in head first and take life on as it comes? There's no sense in guessing what will happen in a month when you can actually just find out. That's more or less what I want to do, I want to find out. I want to "date" for the next month and see what happens. We have that opportunity right in front of us. Now I understand you may feel differently, this is just my side, but it's honest. We could find out in a few short days that we're not right for each other, but at least we can say we tried. Or on the other hand we could realize that we made the perfect decision and when it comes time for you to leave; we may even decide to work through the summer. But these are things I feel like we're already trying to answer when that task is an impossibility. I'm much more of a trial and error person. I can handle having my feelings hurt if it means I gave it a shot right when I wanted to.

There's a lot on my mind. I want to be completely fair to you and tell you exactly what I'm thinking and feeling. This way you can figure out if it makes sense to you and works for you. If it doesn't, then your answer is a whole lot easier, and I could live with that. If we gave this a shot and before you left said it wasn't working, I would feel better than having not given it a shot at all. Because at least we know. With Amanda, things turned out shitty, but at least I know now that she wasn't right for me. It hurt for a bit but it was the best way to figure that out.

I know you said relationships scare you, especially one this soon. Here's how I see it. You know going into it exactly what it entails, and you know who you are going into it with. If this person seems like someone you could see it working with, then it's worth it, if not, then it's not. You're honestly the kind of girl that I could handle a relationship with, so the fact that it "feels like marriage" doesn't really bother me because it's you. It's someone I like and adore, so it's not a terrible thing. If I didn't feel that way, I wouldn't even consider it. So I may not be relationship material to you, in that case it's not worth the shot, but if you like me like you say you do, it shouldn't be much of a problem : )

    Cut and dry, that's just the way I see it. I could really go on for days about you, your personality, your heart and how laying in my bed Wednesday night holding your hand actually gave me butterflies. Kissing you, finally gave me the feeling of what it's like to make the right decision. About how when I'm with you, I am myself, the real me. Not a dumbed-down, watered down version of me. You get everything I say and do and don't ask questions. How laughing with you was a perfect half minute in my life. I'm intense, and I'm passionate, and I'm sure oftentimes it's perceived as naivety and possibly even stupidity, but it's how I live my life. Everything will always be fast paced and given 110 percent. I am sick of thinking, I just want to live. And if that means tomorrow is lived with you in it, I can handle that ;) None the less Allison, you're an undeniably amazing young woman with enormous potential, so thank you for letting me smile.

*Love Always,*
*Jonathan Fisher*

    Alli was moving to New York City a month later. While reading some of these letters after so long, I do realize something about myself, and it's become more apparent in my thirties than any other time in my life, but it's always been there. I live in moments. I know that even if things are going to blow up in my face at some point, it doesn't supersede the want to have an experience. It was almost a foregone conclusion that Alli and I wouldn't work, but I refused to have that inform the decision to not kiss her again, to not laugh with her in my bed, to not live. This is something I've mostly known, but this book has shown it in a direct light for decades of my life.

What I also know is that very few people are on board with my insanity. I honestly think that hearts are meant to be broken. At least mine is. And then it mends, and it moves on, and it loves again. This is my version of beauty. Imagine the moments I would have missed in life if I was worried about a broken heart. I've spent weeks not eating, I know how it feels. And it's still not enough to keep me from experiencing something so rare and beautiful in life--connection. That letter is affirmation.

And so it goes, Alli and I would ultimately decide not to pursue anything beyond those few weeks of hanging out. Alli moved to New York and I felt like it happened the way it was meant to happen. But the romantic in me had other plans. My album still needed one more song, and I was convinced it was going to be for Alli. And that I'd drive to her in New York and play it for her and sweep her off her feet. But that was me, I had no plan beyond that, go figure. So, I sat down at the piano one night in late June of 2007, and this was born.

### I HEART NY
### (Horseshoes and Hand Grenades)

*I came all the way to New York City*
*Just to play this song*
*And hopefully to steal your breath*
*And keep you hanging on to every*
*Word I speak in truthful rhyme*

*Of why I'm really here*
*It's simple but it's realistic*
*It's only for you dear*

*I stayed up late last night and tried to think*
*Of every single line*
*I wanted to write perfection*
*But this is all that I could find*
*And as I sat and read them over*
*Making sure it suited you*
*I was proud to know I wrote the song*
*You've long been overdue*

*And you can watch the sun rise*
*Over everything you know*
*But nothing's real it's only words*
*Until you have been shown*
*So I'm here to keep a promise*
*Let's see what can be made*
*Let's face the facts and move from that*
*Close only counts in horseshoes and hand grenades*

*The subtleties I write are*
*Stinging with my lungs*
*A simple fact, fatal attract*
*To a life that's just begun*
*While the lines on my palms are sweating*
*And my thoughts translate to ink*
*I have a disregard that makes this*
*Harder than you'd think*

*But I'm inching ever closer*
*To the stops I've had in mind*
*And deep breath after deep breaths*
*They're all that I could find*
*So I'll take a risk and ask you*
*Where to go from here*
*I'll be leaving New York City*
*'Cause the road is all too clear*

I never went. I believe it was a long time before Alli even knew I wrote the song, or that it was for her. She inspired words from me that very few others could at a time when they were truly my greatest asset. This would become the title track for the album and one of my favorite songs that I've written to date.

Alli built a wonderful life for herself in New York and still lives there. She seems to have gotten everything she deserves and it absolutely fills me with happiness to see it. A wonderful and happy marriage, a fulfilled life. We've tried to connect on a couple of occasions with my playing in New York, but it hasn't seemed to work yet. I hope the day comes that we get to see each other once again.

Alli saw me as different. She treated me as different. She made sure that she was soft and kind. She supported what I did, believed in my dream, and always had a kind word to offer when I needed one.

Alli, thank you for your inspiration. In my life, I have met few people like you. I'll always remember you as having one of the biggest hearts I've ever known. Thank you for giving yourself to our friendship at such a young age and teaching me all that you did. I hope you feel as though we learned together. I'll never forget these memories, and I know people who will never forget these songs.

Always know that you deserve everything good that comes your way. And that it may be years and miles between us, but I'll always be here rooting you on. I love you.

Alli and me in 2001. Ninth grade.

-Jon-
Hey sweetie! How are you? I'm ok. I'm in a really pissy mood though- haha. Oh- you spelled Allison right here. We haven't talked in like forever! Sorry that I haven't written ya a note for a while, I've been actually doing stuff in my classes! hehe. Aww that sucks that your show got cancelled! I would love to hear you guys at your bar- and I'm pretty sure my mom will let me this time! Haha that's good you are getting your movie! But you aren't ▓▓▓▓▓ hehe. Aww you are so sweet- you are the boyfriend I could ever want! ☺ I know I've asked you this before, but I forgot- are you staying after today? I hope so! Guess what? Yesterday was 2 weeks since the day we started going out! hehe. That's cool about your bro & his g/f! hehe. Well hun, I g/g. I'll ttyl! ☺

~Love Always~
Alli

> Jon,
> HAPPY 2 MONTHS BABY!
> I would have bought you a card but I didn't have a chance to get to a store. Anyways, I just want to let you know how happy I am that we are together! I am so lucky to have you! You are soo+ adorable & sweet & I could go on forever! hehe. Well, I g/g, but I just wanted to tell you all of that. I hope you have a great day! w/B if you want!
> xoxo,
> [signature]

*I found nine of these notes. I picked a couple that I thought were cute.*

**SORRY**
Sorry I'll never meet your standards
Sorry I took the turn
Sorry I never walked your shadow
Sorry you have to learn
That some people just are different from you
Their decisions aren't the same
Sorry some people aren't exactly like you
Sorry you think it's such a shame
Sorry I took my life somewhere
And didn't walk your shoes
Sorry I sang instead of played
Sorry I don't use the things you use
Sorry I might not be like you
But I love my life right now
Sorry I didn't play the game
That you always taught me how
Sorry I'm not what you saw me to be
Sorry I took a different path
Sorry I wasn't the legend you were
I know I make you look like an ass
But I love where I stand right now
Some punk kid in a band
But this punk kid is also in the school play
I know you'll never understand
You overlook what I'm doing right
And see what you think is wrong
But you'll find out some time later
I was doing right all along
I was never good enough for you
I didn't always do what you did
But I rose up and became myself
Maybe I'm not just some punk kid
Sorry I had to tell you this
Sorry you couldn't see
That I'm not you, I'm your little brother
And for now, let ME be ME

*March 18, 2001. I wrote this to my brother Jeff and put it on his bed. We never discussed it.*

# JANELLE & BRET

*June 28, 2001*

*If there was only a way for me to say*
*Everything I felt that day*
*When all my feelings disappear*
*Like you and me were the only ones here*
*Like everything else leaves my head*
*And is completely filled with you instead*
*Like all the functions leave my brain*
*And show me this is not a game*
*But my feelings are strong, my feelings are true*
*My feelings are completely and entirely for you*
*I never thought it could be like this*
*After being apart for a day, it's you I miss*
*And nothing else, nothing more*
*You're the thing worth living for*
*Because it's you, that makes me feel good*
*Do and say things, no one else could*
*And all you say, goes straight to my heart*
*I wish for us to never be apart*
*And to be very close, and be very strong*
*Never fight, and always get along*

> *Be as close as can be, holding you tight*
> *Keeping you safe, away from harm's sight*
> *An untouchable place, that only holds us*
> *A place to be alone and place to discuss*
> *Everything and anything, we need to say*
> *A place where we can just get away*
> *So come to the place I want to be*
> *Janelle, would you go out with me?*
>
> *Love,*
> *Jon*

She said yes. This would prove to be a strange moment in time for one of my best friends and I, her brother, Bret.

It was in the Men's Choir in ninth grade that I met Bret. He was a great guy. He was popular, super charming, and I really looked up to him. He was in the grade above me and this was my first time really interacting with that group of classmates. We would become close very quickly and spend much of our time in similar groups. Chorus guys who were into musicals and who weren't much into the drinking scene.

I believe it was when going to Bret's for a sleepover one weekend that I noticed Janelle. At the time, Janelle was in eighth grade, I was in ninth, and Bret in tenth. I became really close with their entire family. I got along well with their parents, was always cordial with Janelle, but I was there to spend time with Bret and our other friends.

I definitely came to develop a crush on Janelle over the time I spent at Bret's house, but that was always where it stayed. Until Janelle and I had a student council conference together at school at the end of my ninth-grade year. It would be our first real time interacting outside of the "friend's sister" dynamic.

I remember feeling like it was a bit touchy. I was friends with her brother and friends with her parents. As much as it seemed like a fit, it also seemed like a scary chance to take. But I wasn't averse to being an idiot at times, so I asked Bret for his blessing, and I wrote the poem you just read.

It was a strange summer after that because I was at their house often. Sometimes it was in the basement to watch a movie with Janelle, and then other times, it was upstairs with our friends where Janelle "wasn't allowed." So, I just had to kind of wave to my girlfriend and then go hang out with my friend.

Jon,

I thought you would like some pictures of Janelle. I'll send a few and when she finds out she will _kill me_! Have a great week and hope to see you soon!

---

Jon,

When you do something nice, you make it even nicer by adding a warm smile and a word of kindness. No wonder you're appreciated as much as you are!

{Love the smile!}

Thanks Again

Thanks so much for the candy! It was so thoughtful. You are truly a wonderful person.

Love, Robin

---

Jon, I don't know what I can say in this card to make you think to yourself "Man, that kid really cares about me." But all jokes aside, I'll try. You have seriously made such a positive impact on my life Jon. I really and truly can say that I love you with all of my heart. We have to get together this break! Call me whenever you need NETHING!

Happy Holidays

♡ Love you soo much, Bret

These should give you a pretty good idea of the kind of relationship I had with the whole family. Janelle's mom loved that we were together. Bret truly became one of the closest friends I would have in high school. I think I found it to be a lot to handle at that age, but the love was real and felt wonderful.

Janelle was wildly popular and well liked. She had this giant personality that, at times, I didn't even know how to be in the presence of. At school, she made it very apparent that we were a couple and that made me insanely proud, but I also didn't have her confidence. I was actually quite reserved when it came to any kind of PDA. I think now that we were in the same school (ninth and tenth grade were in one building), things became very intense.

I am going to say that it was a week or two before my tenth-grade homecoming that we had a campus-wide student council gathering. There were hundreds of kids from all of the different grades in our high school. There were cameras filming, and the footage was being projected to the front of the auditorium. I was watching the camera pan over all of these kids and then I saw a girl. My jaw dropped. I had no idea who she was, but the only thought in my head was, find out.

This wasn't my most redeeming quality at times, but my need for a challenge was real. In my mind, this was the prettiest girl I think I'd ever seen to that point, and I needed to see if I could find out who she was and get to know her. And that's exactly what I did. I was able to gather some information and find out that her name was Morgan, and that she was in eighth grade. That sounds odd because I was in tenth grade, but remember, I was a year younger. What I came to find out is that we were one year and one day apart.

In one of the least proud moments of my entire life, I ended things with Janelle almost immediately. Again, this being only a week or maybe two before homecoming. I befriended Morgan and had developed a huge crush. It doesn't justify what I did, but in my fourteen-year-old mind, ending it with Janelle was the right thing to do. Everyone was sure to tell me what an asshole I was, and they told me that there was no chance that Morgan's mom would let her go to homecoming with me if I were to ask.

This was just shortly after the attacks on September 11 of 2001. We had a "USA day" or something like that at school. I had bleached my hair often in those days so to be extra patriotic, I permanently dyed my hair half red and half blue. This made the chances of this all coming together even more unlikely. But, true to what I wanted to do, I went to the homecoming parade the week leading up to the dance, and I asked Morgan to go with me. She said yes. We then walked directly over to her mom, so I could meet her and get her blessing. She gave her approval.

The details of that homecoming are truly unimportant beyond Morgan and I going and having a blast. I do remember catching a lot of heat for what I had done, and I think it felt even more traitorous to the girls in my school that I had asked someone who wasn't even in our two grades. But selfishly, it was a perfect night. Morgan and I did not go on to date.

Janelle and I would never really go back to being friends again. Her mom mostly hated me. But somehow, through all of that, Bret and I became even closer. He would remain a very firm fixture in my life and in my circle. I was still trying to figure things out, and he supported me in a big way through all of that.

I actually had a chance to talk to Janelle via Facebook a couple of years ago. She is a doctor, doing amazing work at her school. I haven't talked to Bret in probably fourteen years. Hard to figure out how these things really happen.

I wanted to tell this story because I think being a teenager is messy. This book is meant to be positive and to thank all of those who were in my corner. But it doesn't mean I didn't fuck up at times and that I was incapable of hurting someone. I have my faults, I fought my demons. We're allowed to slip, and we're allowed to make mistakes. What we do with those mistakes is what reveals true character.

Don't ever be afraid to make mistakes.

Janelle and me, summer of 2001.

# KATIE

## Jonny

How can I describe you?
when I'm lost and ready to die
you open up my eyes & take me to a new place
You hold my hand & make me forget
You take the blindness away
& make everything crystal clear
when I fall, you are there to catch me
I can do anything when I'm with you
you set me free.
  Free to laugh, Free to love
  Free to cry, Free to be myself
Just when I thought no one cared
you showed me love
God has a plan for everyone
and He brought you here in my life
to show me what a good friend is
Please never leave my side
Because I can't make it with out you
You are the sweetest person ever
Thank You for giving me a reason
    to be happy
Love Always + Forever,

*My best guess is sophomore year, and I was probably fourteen or fifteen.*

When opening many of the boxes I had found, this letter jumped out at me pretty quickly. It was the very first one that I had read. It stuck out immediately because there was this feeling of pride knowing that a letter like this had all of this effort put into it, and that I was the lucky one on the receiving end. It stuck out even more that I couldn't really remember the circumstances in which this was sent. Were we really that close? I don't remember us dating. This was just friendship. It's what first made me think, maybe I really was making a difference.

I remember being friends with Katie. Although she was three years older than me, we were able to really connect. It makes me insanely proud to look back at a letter like this. Though I haven't spoken to Katie in quite some time, I had to reach out to her and show her what I had found. She seemed genuinely thrilled to see this stuff and was amazed that I still kept it. Then I found more notes, a poem I had written for her, and even some old instant messenger conversations. All of which were able to bring us together a bit after all of these years to discuss high school and our relationship back then.

**February 22, 2001**

*The perfect friend is what I see in you*
*The person I know I can always turn to*
*The person who I will always be there for*
*The one real friend that I truly adore*
*It may seem odd that I turn to you*
*But you're the one who will always be true*
*True to the friendship to which we belong*
*The person with whom I'll always get along*

*The person with whom I never will part*
*The person I have cherished right from the start*
*You didn't have to listen or help me out*
*But you did and that's why I have no doubt*
*In the friendship we hold and stories untold*
*The person to whom my heart can unfold*
*The person who was there when no-one else cared*
*Forever in their eyes I could stare*
*At the starlit sky I see in their eyes*
*The person who never wore a disguise*
*Was always real and was always true*
*I wouldn't be me if I didn't have you!*

Katie and I never dated, though I think I wanted to. I remember feeling that she was out of my league and I never really pursued it much. I do remember taking her to the movies once, but that was the extent of it. No kiss, no follow up, simply friends going out for an evening. But it has led to some awesome follow up and a great way to rekindle some of that friendship. So we have been discussing all of this lately.

As a different approach to these memories, I thought rather than telling my story, I would just kind of pick Katie's brain about it. I asked her why we didn't date, why she felt like she could always come to me, and simply what she remembers in general.

**Katie:** ...music and art can help people and helped us get through any kind of hard or challenging times and you were able to do that for me and I'm sure many others.

**Me:** I obviously cared about you in a big way, and I know it was mutual. I know for me, there was always a sense as to whether it could be more than that at the time. Do you think that was mutual? Like...did we not date for a reason?

**Katie:** I don't think there was any reason. And I obviously felt that way. I've been trying to figure out why we didn't kiss at least?!?!

**Me:** Honestly, me too. So much of my timeline is fleshed out and I understand it. But then there's you, and I kind of lose the detail for some reason. I know for sure I didn't think I could get you. So, I likely didn't make a move out of respect. But, I'm also kind of curious as to why you felt like you could come to me with so much. When you had so many people available to you, why me?

**Katie:** I just always felt a connection with you and really liked you back [then]. It's as simple as that. Not sure why you didn't feel like you could get me. I kinda made it obvious you could haha.

**Me:** I didn't always pick up on obvious. I was sure that you were out of my league. Oftentimes, I was more willing to watch something pass by than make a move and possibly ruin it.

**Katie:** Makes sense.

I really enjoyed this quick discussion. It wasn't only my memory, but both of ours. A conversation to try and work out anything that may have been missed or left out. And furthermore, it brought together the letters I had found in real time and in present day. Hopefully this means that fifteen years won't pass between now and the next time Katie and I talk.

This letter stuck out to me so quickly and in a big way. It helped remind me of the impact I was able to make, and people felt that they could come to me. So much of the inspiration for this book was drawn from this exact letter and others like it.

For that, Katie, I am forever grateful.

Jonny,

Hey! Hala I'm writing you a note. We're taking these ▓▓ tests and I still have like 20 min left & I'm sooo BORED. I miss seeing you soo much. We're hanging out this weekend— I don't care when. So how bout Chris like doesn't talk to me any more. He says like 5 words a day & doesn't call me. I mean if he doesn't like me then he should just tell me & quit hurting my feelings. Ahhh what I would do for a boyfriend like you ☺ Are we still gettin married?! ♡ ur girlfriend— I'm sure everything's good cus ur the nicest guy in the world! I really hope I can make it to ur thing on Sat. If not u'll just have to play the drums for me ru way this weekend. I'm tryin to think of what I did to make things go so wrong w/ Chris right now— All I know is— IT SUCKS. But I still got you so I'm ok ☺. I'm wearin my freaky tiger pants today Hala u gotta love em. I wish I had a hot tub. It would also be cool →

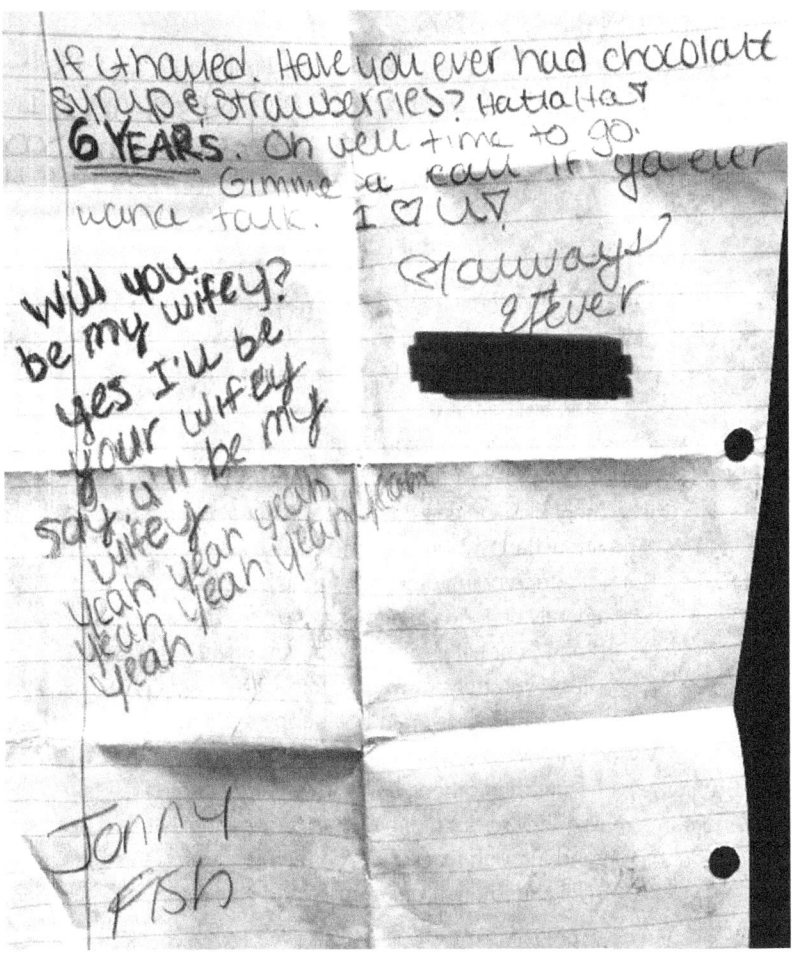

*I love this note from Katie. It's all over the place and really silly but still means so much to me.*

**LIFE**

Someday I hope I figure out
What this thing called life is all about
And I think that day, I'll breathe my last breath
And that is the day, I'll meet my death
Right now it's a journey, through time and through pain
I'm taking my ride on this one way train
'Cause there's no looking back, just pictures and tears
And a few happy moments that pass over years
But not at one point, can you suddenly turn back
And ultimately change all the things you have lacked
Money's not life, it's not what you drive
It's if you truly know how to be alive
And know how to live, and be happy and free
And I know it's a wall everyone of us will see
But some hit harder than others, some land harder when they fall
And some realize they're out of time when they suddenly see it all
Through pain and through tears, through fears and through strife
We've all ended up in this same world called life

September 16, 2002

# NATALIE

**HERE'S A REALLY SILLY MEMORY THAT I HAVE.** In eighth grade, Natalie was new to my world; I barely knew her. But she was one of the most popular girls in school and I thought she was insanely pretty. All my life I have, for some reason, enjoyed trying to punch above my weight. I think I saw this as two-fold. One, I could be fairly confident and feel I had nothing to lose. Two, if it didn't work, I could just say, "Yeah, that went about how I expected."

In true eighth grade fashion, I asked my friend Nick to find out if she liked me. As if he were pulling one over on me, I remember him walking into the gym locker room prior to class and saying, "Hey man, she said she loves you!... as a friend." Okay, fair enough, moving on.

It was probably around ninth grade that Natalie and I became closer friends. We definitely ran in similar circles at times, but she was also one of the most appealing girls in our entire school, so getting her time or attention was no easy task. She was tall and very pretty, the without makeup kind of pretty. She also had the most amazing singing voice. The friendship was perfectly fine by me. I honestly thought that if I was going to let one girl slide off my radar, it might as well be her.

I was a pretty weird kid. I look back, and I think I was pretty cool, but I'm not convinced. I could be charming, and I was aware enough to not be socially awkward. But I was a chorus geek who wore bizarre things to school and who tended to march to the beat of his own drum, and I don't think it was always that rhythmic. The point is, I think this actually helped me. I think it worked.

I had this insane obsession with the Olsen twins. And it was no secret. I owned their movies, magazines, books, dolls, stickers, posters. You name it, I owned it. Everyone thought it was this adolescent obsession with pretty twins, but I watched every movie! I would have what I called "Jon days," where I would skip school and just lay in bed all day. It was a mental recharge. And sometimes on those days, I would spend ten hours watching their movies. They were easy to watch, no drama or stress, always a happy ending. It was part of my therapy.

Anyway, Natalie and I grew closer over that year and the summer after ninth grade, we became very close. We shared a mutual friend and the two of them were always together. They'd show up at my house, and it was always a blast. One night, I was lying on the couch in my living room and they came bursting in with a poster of the latest Olsen movie. They had just stolen it from the local movie theater. So yeah, that kind of thing.

---

**June 8, 2001**

**J Dawg Fish:** Hey1 Guess What?!?!
**LFu▮▮54:** what??
**J Dawg Fish:** I Love you!:-D
**LFu▮▮54:** hehehehehe I LOVE YOU TOO!!!! :-)
**J Dawg Fish:** yay:-) eheh
**J Dawg Fish:** I wanna see what u wrote1
**LFu▮▮54:** haha do you want me to typw it to you?

**LFu▮▮54:** type*
**J Dawg Fish:** I dont know, kause i'm kinda scared to send u mine
**LFu▮▮54:** awww you don't have to if you don't want to! you might be scared by mine too!!
**LFu▮▮54:** its kinda werid
**J Dawg Fish:** Go ahead, I'll suck it up and send mine:-) hehe
**LFu▮▮54:** alright! it might take a few
**LFu▮▮54:** hold on!!
**J Dawg Fish:** Its kool1 hehe, gives me time to cusk up my fear, Haha
**J Dawg Fish:** suck*
**LFu▮▮54:** Jon fisher! wow what an incredible guy! seriuosly the way he is and everything about him is so awesome but also so interesting. Its like he has so much emotion and feeling for things and he loves to express himself is so many different ways and that is so awesome! But its also like he has this secret that he is hidding from everyone and there is this mysterious side to him. It draws me to want to know everything about him! I don't think he knows this but ever since we have been getting to know eachother better and becoming better friends he has always been so interesting to me. He wants to be good at the things that he does and he is good at them! I guess in a way i wish i could be like him! I hope that we stay in eachothers lives for a very very long time because it just the little time we have been friends he has taught and showed me how to be a better person without even trying to just by being himself. I don't think people realize what a great person he really is. there are so many fake people out there and there are so many people with so many different sides that you don't know which one is really them, but its sooo different with jon its like what you see is what you get and there is nothing fake about him he is sooo real and i love that! I just wish i could have gotten to know him earlier because he is sucha special person to have in my life
**LFu▮▮54:** :-\ hehe now i am kinda embarrassed
**J Dawg Fish:** Wow, Natalie, i'm speechless
**LFu▮▮54:** that is word for word! haha :-\
**J Dawg Fish:** Aww, that has to be one of the sweetest things i've heard, and it means so much to me
**LFu▮▮54:** really good! because i don't think you know how great you are sometimes!
**J Dawg Fish:** I think u might give me a little too much credit, but thats okay:-) hehe, um... your gonna totally look at me in a different light and maybe see me as a whole different person after u see the poem
**LFu▮▮54:** awwwww as long as it is not a bad light im sure it won't! unless you want it to
**J Dawg Fish:** I kant believe i'm sending this...
**J Dawg Fish:** Natalie
When I think of this girl, I could almost cry

She constantly has me wondering why
Why God put such amazing people on this earth
The world suddenly changed on the day of her birth
And since the day I met her, I so easily know
This is a person, I could never let go
Cause she means so much, and is just so great
I am so blessed to know her, maybe it's fate
Or at least that's what I'd like it to be
Cause this girl can just suddenly set me free
Free from any care, I have in the world
This isn't just an ordinary girl
She's not a girl, I can just pass by
And I'm probably stupid, for giving a try
But I know I just have to, I have to be brave
I want to know 100%'s what I gave
Because she's worth so much, just with that smile
For her I would aimlessly walk for miles
As long as I knew, that when I was done
I could have her, as my only one
It's just her attitude, and her gorgeous looks
Someone you couldn't find, even in books
She's just so much more, than anyone can write
I think of her daily, and always at night
Go beyond fairy tales, beyond your dreams
That's where she'll be, and that's why she means
So much to me, and now I know
She's definitely a person I could never let go
At least as friend, I'd hope her for more
Cause she's just a person, I truly adore
But for now she's taken, so I'll sit and wait
See if there is, a such thing as fate
And see if Miss Perfect, will ever be mine
Maybe we'll see, only in time
So I just thought I'd write, all that I felt
Cause this girl's just beautiful, she makes my heart melt
I truly do love her, As a great friend
Maybe even more, we'll see in the end

**J Dawg Fish:** Maybe not what u expected....
**LFu████54:** Jon....
**LFu████54:** you just made me cry
**LFu████54:** that is the most wonderful thing anyone in the entire world has ever said to me or written to me
**LFu████54:** thank you so much you don't even understand
**LFu████54:** i don't look at you differently at all! well not in a bad way!!!

**J Dawg Fish:** Like i said, everything i ever write is true, and it komes straight out of my heart, u kan maybe see y i was hessitant to send it, but i had to kause now u know how i exactly feel
**J Dawg Fish:** And your very welcome
**LFu▮▮54:** I LOVE YOU JON!!!!! :-)
**J Dawg Fish:** I LOVE YOU TOO NATALIE!!!!!:-)
**LFu▮▮54:** :-) now we have this bond!! i love it!!
**J Dawg Fish:** I know:-) wow, I've never felt so klose to anyone! Besides Jon, and u know what he means to me, i feel like i've known you forever
**LFu▮▮54:** I know!!! yea i know how much jon means to you and that is awesome that you two have that! i know like we are soul mates in a way or something!
**J Dawg Fish:** Ya, Thats awesome!
**J Dawg Fish:** Like, even before all this, like when Alli and i got in those big fights, who did i kall to cry to? You, theres just always been somt5hing about you
**LFu▮▮54:** You don't know how happy i am that you can come to me when you need to talk to someone or just need to be there! And especially when its you that needs the help i was always more then willing!
**J Dawg Fish:** I'm very happy that i have someone like u to turn to, kause u r real, i'll always know i'm turning to the real Natalie ▮▮▮▮▮
**LFu▮▮54:** Aww thanks and i will always know that i am turning to the real and ONLY Jon Fisher!
**J Dawg Fish:** Aww:-D
**LFu▮▮54:** I know a song we can sing!!! its a classic!!
**J Dawg Fish:** What song?
**LFu▮▮54:** Ain't No Mountain High Enough!
**J Dawg Fish:** do u have it on Napster?
**LFu▮▮54:** haha no! you know what song it is don't you?
**J Dawg Fish:** Ya, but i dont know it really weel
**LFu▮▮54:** well i will see you before wednesday and i will help you out! :-)
**J Dawg Fish:** Okay:-)
**J Dawg Fish:** how will u see me before wed.?
**J Dawg Fish:** oh HEY!
**LFu▮▮54:** what?
**LFu▮▮54:** we just will
**J Dawg Fish:** Please come to my game Teusday, i kan take you! It's in Mrs, which is pretty klose to C-berry, and i think im pitching
**LFu▮▮54:** OMG i want to go soo bad! it is my parents 24 anniversary and they are taking me and my bro out to eat down town and i don't want to go at all :-( i would rather go to your game in a heart beat!
**LFu▮▮54:** what time is your game?
**J Dawg Fish:** Awwww, its fine:-) thats a happy occasion, go!:-) i'll have more games
**LFu▮▮54:** ok but that makes me soo mad because i had a feeling some-

> thing would be going on that day when my mom said that i couldn't do anything!
>
> Auto response from J Dawg Fish: One Sec! Sorry Nat, please stay on:-)
>
> **LFu▪▪54:** k :-)
> **J Dawg Fish:** its fine:-) they're will be more games:-)
> **LFu▪▪54:** sorry i was brushing my teeth :-D i am determined to see one of your games when you pitch though!!
> **J Dawg Fish:** Okay:-)
> **LFu▪▪54:** well jon i am very tired! but this was one of the best talks :-) thanks for being soo awesome! I love you!! and ill tty tomorrow!
> **LFu▪▪54:** signed off at 12:31:33 AM.

*These are so damn embarrassing. I swear I'm actually the one writing this book. In proper English.*

That would be the final summer that I would play real organized baseball. I was a fairly decent baseball player, and that year I got put on an amazing team. We went to the playoffs, and the town rallied behind us. True to her word, so did Natalie and Jess. I don't think they missed a single playoff game! They even had shirts made that said something like "Jon is" followed by a flame. It had my number on the back.

*Well, I found the picture! "Jon is hot," with the flame, of course. Natalie is top right.*

I had a real chance to shine on the field in front of my friends, family, peers, and the coolest girl in school. It was one of the most fun months of my entire life. I'll always remember it fondly for so many different reasons. It was the best season I ever played, it was the first and only homerun I would ever hit in my life, and I was able to do it amongst close friends and great coaches. Ultimately, in game three of a three-game series, we would go on to win the championship. That picture was from the night that we won. What a great group of guys and an unbelievable memory.

Going into tenth grade, Natalie and I were always talking and hanging out. We were both single for a time after my whole homecoming fiasco with Janelle, and I still kind of held out on pursuing anything. I remember some of the phone calls we would have where we would talk about who we liked. I always dreamed she'd one day say my name during that conversation. Instead, she started dating one of my best friends, Bret. Yeah, that Bret.

True to Bret being there for me when I needed, I did my best to do the same for him and Natalie. I was happy to see them together. I tried to make sure that as long as two people close to me were happy, I'd be happy for them. But truthfully, it didn't last long between them. And as I'm going over this in my head, this timeline actually seems quite crazy.

Homecoming was probably in early October of tenth grade, so 2001. Janelle and I came crashing down, as you know. Natalie and Bret continued to date during all of this. And within what must have been the next month or two, they broke up. Wow, we all really bounced around I guess.

After Natalie and Bret broke up, I officially found myself wanting to pursue her. But I was hesitant, and didn't want to mess anything up, so I was patient. I bided my time by being a good friend, being there for her, and making the most of our time together. Just as we were going into Christmas break, things really seemed to be ramping up.

One night, during Christmas break (I found that this was December 29), I went to Natalie's house to hang out and exchange some Christmas gifts. We were simply going to watch some movies and talk. We were in her basement, I was on the futon and she was on the floor sitting in front of me. Turning from the screen to talk, Natalie and I kind of locked eyes and both went in for our first kiss. This was maybe as stunned as I'd been to date by a situation unfolding. I can tell you now that I think this would be the catalyst for much of the growth in my teenage years. For better and for worse.

After the kiss, Natalie just looked at me and said, "So... what are we?" *How is this happening? How is this girl asking me what we are? Whatever the hell you want us to be!* I said, "I'm not really sure. We should just be together." And so we were. I walked out of Natalie's front door that evening, with my collared shirt under my sweater, like I was on top of the entire world. How I got there, I didn't know. But I did, and the rest didn't seem to matter.

Natalie and I absolutely hit the ground running. We were inseparable; we were committed. What I had always wanted out of a relationship, I was now getting. Real dates, real thought, real time, and real dedication. I'm not saying it was healthy, I'm just saying what it was. We spent so much of our free time together. We came of age together.

The entire school knew we were dating. Teachers knew. It was kind of strange. We were "that" couple. Annoyingly in love, selfishly connected.

Sometime around May of tenth grade, so about four to five months later, we were on a chorus trip together. Natalie broke up with me for a couple of days during that trip. That sounds so ridiculous but I say it for a reason. When that happened, I think she was overwhelmed. I think she was seeing how this was getting serious, and she got scared. I will never forget the amazing support system I had around me during that trip to get me through such a painful time. By the time we got home from the trip, we were back together.

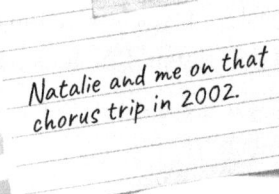

Natalie and me on that chorus trip in 2002.

Natalie is almost exactly a year older than me. One year and eight days to be exact. This means that in October of tenth grade, she was able to get her permit and was driving alone by June. Her parents bought her a brand-new Volkswagen Jetta and she got a crazy allowance each week for gas and whatever the hell else she might want. So, imagine that. The summer after tenth grade we had a car, plenty of money, and a fierce obsession.

I recall the summer fairly well. She would pick me up, we'd go to her house, we'd hang out all day, she'd drive me home. Rinse and repeat. If there was a party, we might go, but if we did it was going to be together. We alienated our friends and seemed to have had tunnel vision. We were going to be prom king and queen, go to college together, be high school sweethearts. The whole thing.

But we fought like idiots. Neither of us was able to handle what this was no matter how hard we tried. The jealousy was insane, the arguments were petty but fierce. We would say things we would later regret. And then we would make up and move on, leaving scars the entire way. We were kids in an adult relationship. If there was ever a cautionary tale about really dating in high school, we were it.

Here's where I think my head was. I had somehow managed to get what I considered to be the best girl in school. I don't think I always knew how to handle that. I didn't like when she talked to certain guys, I didn't like that she was a trainer on the football team. This was my wildest of insecurities as a fifteen-year-old navigating this for the first real time.

Like I said, Natalie was insanely talented. At a time, she was getting guitar lessons. We would go together and I would just pal around the shop while she was in her lesson. The kid who worked the counter? Our age, insanely attractive, and a better musician than I was. We fought about it constantly. At the same time, I was asked to a Sadie Hawkins dance by a girl from the grade above me (Natalie couldn't have attended since it wasn't in our school) and I said yes. She was simply a friend, but it was wildly unfair of me in hindsight.

And just as I would do to her, Natalie would make sure I heard about it. Then we would simply repeat a fight we'd had plenty of times before. These are moments that I truly wonder if I would take back. Were we learning or doing harm? She didn't deserve that. I didn't deserve that.

By the time eleventh grade rolled around, it was her and I. She would pick me up for school and drop me off after. We met between classes; we couldn't get enough. I remember homecoming that year, one of the two years that I actually danced with the one that brought me. We had plans to go with a big group of friends who, at the last minute, removed us from their plans citing not wanting to "watch us fight the whole time." We were losing the world around us and never thought to care.

We would make the best of that homecoming, I remember. Deciding that the actions of our friends only meant that we had to be even closer and stronger for one another. We had hibachi for dinner, she paid. We went to the dance and had a blast. We had a sleepover at her house with snacks and movies; it was perfect. Us against the world, but that sits on a house of cards.

Within a month or two after, I invited Natalie to my house on a Friday night following a football game. We sat in my living room, and I told her that I didn't think we should be together anymore. How did it get to that point? How did I become the guy breaking up with the girl I never thought I'd get? This struck me as a surreal moment. Also, this did not go well. Natalie started throwing pillows at me, crying, and struggling to keep herself together. I'm not saying I blame her, I knew how devastating this was going to be for the both of us, but I felt like it had to be done.

Shortly after, we would take another stab at things. If I had to guess, it was within a week or two. I think jealousy got the best of me with all of the new attention she was getting, and I broke down. However, in February of 2003, it really did end. It ended horribly and without friendship. In hindsight, I'm not surprised. The intensity of that relationship at that age almost guaranteed disaster when it came crashing down. We barely spoke; our friends got kind of weird, but we eventually moved on.

I have a memory in my head from when I was about six or seven years old. It is of my brother Jeff sitting in a balled-up position, his knees tucked to his chest, against the third-floor hallway wall. He was on the phone and crying uncontrollably. I didn't know what was going on. I would come to find out that he was being broken up with by his high school sweetheart after about three years.

I bring that memory up because I eventually lived it. And what I realize is that we all do, or most of us. The end of our first love. Sure, it was my decision, but it didn't hurt any less, or mean any less. It crushed me; it crushed Natalie. I was sixteen years old and really had to figure out how to cope with that emotion. Truth is, I probably didn't handle it so well. However, I know it built character. And for me, that is worth the pain.

Memories are faulty. Even with all of these notes, poems, and letters that I have, my memory is sure to fail me at times. Up until twenty minutes ago, when I found a poem that was titled strangely, I had completely forgotten that Natalie would come into my life one last time. So, let's just take this ride together. What I try and do before I write is gather up everything I can to inspire the story I'm about to tell. Well, I did that with Natalie but one fell through the cracks. Again, twenty minutes ago, here's what I found…

## THINGS I'VE LEFT UNSAID
### (Perfection)

*I know I could stare in your eyes for hours*
*And get lost within the text*
*Forgetting that time is brushing me by*
*And that maybe my life is a mess*
*You do that to me, you give me that thrill*
*You hand me a place to escape*
*And if you'd allow me I'd stay there*
*Until there was nothing between us to say*
*But even then I think I'd allow myself*
*To let you not let me go*
*Allow me to wander through your perfections*
*And the things that are hidden below*
*The surface of an angel that you call your skin*
*Blessed with a beauty and charm*
*An adorable face only fit for a king*
*That I know could never be harmed*
*I see things inside you that many don't see*
*Even beyond your beautiful looks*
*Things I may have even discovered*
*You don't even find those things in books*
*Your humor and swift personality*
*Your graceful ability to laugh*
*At even yourself and some things that you do*
*I love you and will never take it back*
*So thank you for giving me something*
*That has given me strength to forget*
*Or at least set aside the life at my door*

*And be thankful that we could have met*
*You're perfect, you're flawless, impeccable*
*Faultless, superb, and supreme*
*And every day that I've spent with you*
*I've felt I was living a dream*
*Happy Valentine's Day to perfection*
*I hope you don't mind that name*
*Cause when I see the definition and look in your eyes*
*It seems to be one in the same*

*Happy Valentine's Day Natalie!*
*I love you!*
*~Love Always and Forever~*
*-Jonathan-*

Okay, so I do have to rely on technology here, and when I check the file info, it says that this was created on February 14, 2005 at 2:01 AM. So I started to wonder... how did this get that time stamp? Valentine's day seems right, that part matches. And now I have a slight bit of memory coming back.

There was a time in college when Natalie's parents were away for a weekend. I have no idea how it came to be but I went to her house and spent the night. I remember watching *The Girl Next Door*. I don't remember much else from that evening. I do, however, remember Natalie coming to see me at college once. I remember this because I introduced her to my roommate, he stumbled all over his words and then ran out the door. Shortly after, he came back to the room with a friend. Later he would say, "I had to show people the girl you brought into our room, I thought she was a model." Which I find to be hilarious and very kind. And, thanks to him, I have that memory.

I also am finally putting together that this must be where the following letter fits in…

Jon,

You asked me to not bite my tongue and say what I wanted to say, but I don't want to let you in to a place that I swore I would never let you see again. Do you have any idea how many times you crossed my mind and how many times I had to shut my eyes, to all the things that reminded me of you? I don't think you do, or was it the same for you? Did you wait by the phone at midnight and stare at it straight through sunrise waiting for nothing?

Well, it doesn't matter now. Your face erased the year gone by and all the times I cried. Never mind, I don't want you to know that I cried for you. But, I can't help to look in your eyes and wonder if you did the same because you missed me. You were never one to cry, but I know you wanted to. I know everything about you, I know about the nights you stay awake and how scared you are, I know who you are. The year has changed me, but you can still see what no one sees. What does it mean?

Out of you and me, you're the thinker, so you have the answer. It's not that easy. We found that out the hard way, thinking you didn't need to kiss me. I don't need your hands on my neck, but I need it. I want it, just like I don't want your lips so close to mine, but I'm lying and you know it. Do you remember my hands fitting so perfectly behind your head, pulling you in? Think about this. I forgot how much I did.

I'm sorry, so sorry, I didn't intend for this story to write it self like it did. But I did think I could be your friend, so much for good intentions. Nevertheless, we can't help but laugh, and your laugh sets me at ease because it makes me see that you are just as screwed up as me. I am not alone because you are there, and that's all that's in focus. I couldn't tell you about the view when dawn broke; I'm sure it was beautiful, but my eyes will stuck in close up to yours, and that would make even the cloudiest Sunday morning one to sit and admire.

But back to this, what does it all mean? I don't really know, but for the time being I am enjoying the adventure. Now go be you and ill be me, and when you think of me picture that second before you kissed my lips, the feeling of my breath, and in that moment how nothing was wanted more. When I see you that will all be real and all the want will rush from you to me and me to you.

I'm not sure if I want you to actually have the chance to know all of this, but I'm guessing you had an idea. It is what it is, which gets us back to nowhere. We are useless with no control. And right now that's all I know.

~Natalie

I remember this letter because it is so beautifully crafted. I was, and still am, convinced that she was trying to be poetic, and she truly nailed it. But what I remember most about this letter is that second to last line, "We are useless with no control." It is such a great line and kind of an appropriate ending to the letter. I remember being floored by this.

As I said before, Natalie was absolutely overflowing with talent. She could sing better than any girl in our grade, she played guitar, she was vibrant and smart. So, it shouldn't be a shock to see such a bright young woman write something so well. I was lucky to be on the receiving end of it.

That line stuck in my head so much that I just took a stab and typed it into the search on my hard drive. Here's what came up ... one file.

*We are useless with no control*
*And right now that's all I know*
*And if you're guessing I stole these words from you*
*Just go ahead and say so*

Apparently I felt it should be a song. Though an incomplete one. I wrote that "note" on April 11, 2005. Thus, completing this insane timeline that we got to travel together. This is why I'm doing this and this is why I want you here with me as I do.

Natalie and I dated for a little over a year when we were about fifteen to seventeen years old. She was my "high school sweetheart," and I was hers. Every girl that would follow after her for years to come would be up against that baseline. We weren't perfect, but we sure as hell learned a lot, taught a lot, and grew a lot. I should have been better to Natalie; the whole thing could have been better. But my hope is that we took what we learned and we grew from it.

Though Dana is the first girl I believe I ever truly loved, Natalie was the first girl I fell in love with. Everyone has one of those, and everyone needs one.

Natalie is happily married today, actually to an old friend of mine from high school. I don't think we've spoken since we were about nineteen but I still think back fondly on our time together and hope that she can pull positives from it just as I always try to do. Natalie supported my music and believed I could be a success. Actually, for senior superlatives, we were the male and female recipients of "Most Likely To Be Famous." Who knows, maybe we still can be.

Natalie, thank you for all of the amazing scrapbooks. Thank you for accepting me playing drums shirtless with red hair and for painting my nails black before my shows. Thank you for being a fan when I always needed one. Thank you for your patience and tolerance, and thank you for your artistry. You'll always be this giant memory in my life, and I will always hope for the very best for you. From my heart to your hands.

**DREAM AWAY**

When I open my eyes
My dreams fall short
A simple setback
To a major reward
Sort of sleeping
Yet feeling it all
Seems so real
In a world so small
Eyes wide shut
Breathing gains speed
Paints a picture
Called a masterpiece
If I could sleep
All day I would
This paradise carries
My every word
Don't have to speak
Don't have to move
My dream will take me
I'll be consumed
Don't interrupt
Let me lay
Let me dream
My life away

July 7, 2002

## SOLITARY CONFINEMENT

All my life I've been on a mission
To not be kept in my own damn prison
Where I'm the warden and can't let me escape
If I could keep myself in confinement
Where solitude was my last apartment
And the only light I saw was the light in your eyes

Then my jail cell would be freedom
My footsteps half a mile
To where I want to go
And be myself for a while
Where I'm not just a number
And I'm not just a slave
Where the air I breathe is all mine
And it's free for the take

The cold walls creep into my silence
And I retreat in spite of my vengeance
And let the soft concrete echo out your name
I want to touch your hand and engage it
Let you know you're what my mind created
When I was younger, and pictured my last breath

And every day draws closer
To the day I won't return
Where hypocrites like me
Are none of your concern
Shadows they try to mock me
For the teardrops from my eyes
And the shattered glass that falls around me
Falls at my demise

January 27, 2003

*The first song I ever officially wrote with music.*

# JESS

THIS STORY IS HERE FOR ONE MAIN REASON, because people make mistakes, and when we do, we need support from others to remind us that forgiveness and love are real.

Jess and I became friends in chorus in tenth grade; she was a grade above me. This is the trip during which Natalie and I would go through some difficulties. I was turning in whatever direction I could, and some amazing friends were holding me up. I think Jess and I became much closer on that weekend than we ever had before.

Jess and me on a chorus trip in 2002.

But really, this story is about the end of Jess's senior year. May of 2003. A group of us went to see *Finding Nemo* and Jess and I did the whole high school flirt thing. With graduation coming up and Jess headed to Kentucky for college, it was an odd time to start something up. But I really enjoyed her company, and so we hung out more.

I remember a Sunday night, it must have only been a week or so later, I went to Jess's house as our first time further exploring these feelings. I really always wanted to impress Jess, she brought that out of me. I remember going to her house when she wasn't home and asking her mom for her car keys, so I could sneak things in there. The night of her graduation I put a book, flowers, and a note on her doorstep for her to come home to.[7]

Only a week or two after this, I was heading on a vacation with my friends who were graduating; it was their senior trip. I remember having all of these silly conversations with Jess prior to my leaving where she would say, "Don't kiss any girls," or something like that. I remember us doing that a lot, projecting our insecurities. Trust me, I did the same to her. I obviously told her I wouldn't do that, and she had nothing to worry about. I'm sure you can gather, it didn't go as planned.

We went to the Outer Banks, and truly just went to spend time together and enjoy the week. Bret was there and it was the first time he'd really ever asked me about dating his sister. I don't know why I remember that or why he waited so long, but that's what happened. And it was hilarious. Anyway, it was our first or second night there and we decided to go to a dance club. Why? That's one thing I

---

[7] Not knowing shit about how the other half lived, I never realized that people rarely use their front doors, they always used the garage. So about two hours after she got home and not hearing from her, I eventually had to call her and ask her to go to her front door. Much less slick, but the point was made.

cannot answer today.

We were at this place, I want to seriously say it was called "The Pit," but maybe that's my memory deciding that's what it should be called. Or maybe you're reading this and thinking *holy shit, I've been there!* Because my guess is that if you were sixteen to nineteen and in the Outer Banks, this is the kind of place you just end up.

I was standing and talking to a friend when I noticed a girl standing alone on the other side of the dance floor. Very cute, very unassuming. I walked over and said "Why aren't you dancing?" You know, like a badass. I think she said something like she didn't know, and I probably said something stupid like "Well, you should be." I grabbed her hand. We danced. Her name was Hannah.

Shortly after I got home from that trip, I apparently did some writing. Because I just typed the name Hannah into my search and found this…

**June, 2003**

*Now to the most important of things from this trip, Hannah ▮▮▮▮▮▮▮. She was a girl I met at a dance club (my first time ever at one). I saw her the whole night and told all my buddies about how cute I thought she was. So, after about an hour of thinking, I asked her to dance. She said yes, we got to be friends, exchanged numbers, and so on. I do have a girlfriend but it wasn't any big deal to meet this girl, it's just nice to get to know people. We called and talked and what not, and came to realize our houses were only three miles or so apart. Me and my friends figured hanging out with her and the three girls she was with, wasn't such a bad idea. The first night we went to see them, they were pretty lit up (alcohol) so we left. That's a bad situation and we wanted no part of it. Well, here comes the next night, the four girls come over to our house for a little get together and hanging out. Hannah and I get to talking and both state that we have significant others. She, on the other hand, had basically said that she liked me and wasn't too worried about her boyfriend back home. I said I'd never cheat on a girl, so her and I decided it would be best to not mess things up. We drove around a while and talked and enjoyed ourselves, but it happened anyway. We went back to my house, laid together for a while and I ended up kissing her. I thought I would feel like hell afterwards, but I feel like it was a smart decision, she was a beautiful, nice girl, and shit, I'm only sixteen years old. Now, I know you may say I'm an asshole for saying it was smart, but I have NEVER done something I would consider completely against my beliefs, and this did. Not in a bad way, just going against what I thought was morally right and instead, doing what I wanted. She was a different sort of girl, not one that I often would show interest in, nonetheless, I did. So that was... Wednesday, I met her Monday just for your knowledge.*

*Thursday they came back over, but that night didn't go so well, my roommates ended up not liking her so much and she and them got in a fight, and I had to be the mediator. Fortunately, all's well that ends well; I said goodnight that night and partied again with the boys.*

*Now for Friday, the reason I'm writing all this. This wasn't some girl I had like fallen in love with, you know? It was some stupid little crush from vacation. She had said she liked me a little, I felt that way also, so whatever. We wanted to see each other before we left Saturday morning so we got together for a while Friday night. We sat and talked for a while, got to know each other more, exchanged numbers, screen names, e-mail addresses, that whole deal. And alas, goodbye crept in. It was time to say goodbye, and come to terms that we will most likely never see each other again. I'm a bit of a sappy* romantic, I watch stupid movies just because they're cute and have happy endings. I will elaborate at some point later but anyway, this was sort of my fairy tale, and it was time to say goodbye to it. Movies are easy, they just end it on a happy note and roll the credits. I can't roll credits, I had to leave. I gave her one more kiss goodnight, drove her and her friend home, and said goodbye to the rest of the people at her house (we met their parents, cousins, etc.). Driving home Friday night from their house was the kicker. I hadn't realized until that point the crush I had developed for her. Not like love, or marriage shit, it was just too perfect to say goodbye. I met a nice girl, got to know her, and after 5 days, said goodbye. It's rough, and that's the first time I've ever really done it.

It's time now for me to pour my heart out into my keyboard and tell y'all my feelings. I told only one roommate about this, and we had a great talk. I can confide in him, and he was the only other one who liked her. By the way, It was Justin who I talked about before. He handled it great, was a good talker and helped out a lot; I just had to tell someone. Now it's time to say everything else that I would just not like to tell anyone but Hannah. This is my escape, so all opinions and things are absolutely necessary so I will just ramble on about this girl for a while. What I hope now is that she is on her plane bound for Colorado (that's where she lives) thinking exactly what I'm thinking. That is something like… I miss her, I hope she felt like I did, and I hope I made a difference in her vacation like she did in mine. I want her to take a piece of me home with her and keep it, as I did. Something I worry about is her going home and forgetting about me, because I don't like "hook-ups," they're just not me. I always have this attachment (minor at least) that is emotional. I developed feelings, nothing too major, but I did. I truly hope she feels the same way, that I wasn't just some hook-up, but a nice guy she met on vacation and won't forget. We said that maybe someday we could find a way to meet again, or something of that nature. How realistic that is, who knows. She worried I was going to go home thinking I made a mistake and would forget about her. That makes me feel good because it shows that she cared about how I felt, which is a plus. I'm aware I look like a big asshole writing all this having a girlfriend, but it's circumstantial and hard to explain, so as like most things, I'll get to that later. I'll also check in and let you know how things go with her and I talking or what not. I haven't been keeping up with this lately so I will try harder now that schools out and such. Hannah was a great girl, and I have definitely come home with one great souvenir, a friendship.

 As for the having a girlfriend thing. I'll explain my side of the story as best to give you a look at how I might observe the situation. Let it first be stated that I morally never do anything that might challenge my values. So I would have never done it had I felt it was absolutely outrageous to do what I did. My "girlfriend" and I are sort of dating you could say. We never made anything official but we had talked about our vacations and what not. I told her I was going into the vacation having a girlfriend figuring that no girl would ever start to like me or anything like that. I may not always have the highest self-esteem but I've never really met girls on vacations and stuff and I figured it wouldn't happen there, but it did. Hannah and I started talking about it and it took me a good part of two hours to finally decide to do what I wanted to do. If I didn't want to do it, I never would have, but I did. I figured, I'm sixteen, I just had a thirteen month relationship end, and it's a good chance for me to finally have a little fun. I normally don't do things that are out of the ordinary, mostly because I'm afraid to step out of my zone. I actually feel quite proud that I did it because I made a decision based on how I felt and what I wanted to do, instead of what's wrong and right. So step into my shoes for a bit, give me a chance to plead my case, and don't just come out calling me an asshole until you see how I feel. Okay, against what I thought I would do, I called my girlfriend last night, her name is Jess by the way, and confessed. I told her I kissed somebody on vacation. There were a lot of awkward pauses that followed and by the time I went to bed and she did also, nothing got accomplished. I was hoping she would just like call me an asshole and what not and tell me how she felt. Rather, she was just silent. She said she wasn't pissed, but hurt. It's about this time that I start wondering If I still made the right decision, and I come to you to spill out all the things I bring into play. Jess and I had something pretty good. There wasn't much base for it, like a structure but how it was going when I left was good. I missed her when I left and the first few days of the trip I missed her. Towards the end of the trip, I found myself not wanting to go home. I didn't not want to go home just because of Jess, I just didn't want to leave my week in Heaven. I am not one to sacrifice another's feelings to make myself happy. I NEVER put myself in front of others. I never have, it's just how I approach things. Figures the first time I do I hurt somebody and feel extremely bad about it. I did what I wanted to do, and never took into consideration how it might affect others. I did I guess, but came to the conclusion that I needed to finally, for once, put myself ahead and live life a little. I guess I'm still glad I did it, I just now feel awful for hurting Jess. Hopefully it all passes over, she eventually forgives me, and I still feel okay about doing what I did. Not okay like forget how Jess feels, but to the extent that it didn't ruin her life (which I'm sure it didn't) and I still feel that it was time for me to worry about myself.

I had no idea I was going to include that in this book; I barely remember writing it, but I might as well share it because it exists.

Jess and I would stay in touch after that and remain friends. This is why I started this story the way I did. Because she was better than me in those moments. But if I was going to learn anything, it was going to have to be that way, because I made a mistake. Jess was different. She saw the world in a different way and I always felt like I could have these amazing and intellectual conversations with her.

Jess left for college, and I started my senior year of high school. I got the following letter on November 8, 2003.

> Jonathan Fisher                                                    11-5-03
> 
> heeeey! Isn't this cool? I'm writing you a note... and then mailing it haha. How's your day going? I'm in psychology... and I'm not really paying attention to our 2-week discussion of sex anymore, so you are the lucky one who gets el note. ☺
> What fun exciting stuff is going on at Seneca? I miss the people (well like 5 of them) but college is so much nicer-no busywork kinda crap assignments & stuff. Such as... senior project! what are you doing for yours anyway, do you know yet? Oh & when are musical tryouts? Don't worry, you will do wonderful!! ☺ Class president AND the lead of the musical... you just need to add like prom king or something to your list hehe. Or maybe just being famous will be enough... ☺
> Anything fun going on there this weekend? I'm housesitting for my old neighbors b/c they're going to Cincinnati, and Katie & my friend Abby are staying with me too, so it will be fun ☺ I'll be hanging out with Marc Broussard alll weekend, since that's like my new life obsession... hehe.
> hm... my life is kinda boring, I really don't have much to tell you? Except that I want you to meet the Olsens! haha. And then when you are this big famous musician, I'll be like hey-we used to be friends before he decided to be too cool and forget about me... haha. My life is really un-exciting, I'm sorry, I have no fun stories to tell you! Hopefully my life will be more fun & I'll have good stories at Thanksgiving. I can't wait til Christmas break, just to have a break from doing work and studying! Mmm I've successfully not taken a single note today & class is over yaaay! ☺ I love you & I miss you & hopefully I'll get to see you when I'm home!
>                                                                   ♡ Jess
> 
> PS. I want a sr. pic of yours now!! ☺

This note makes me emotional. She had forgiven me, shown compassion, and decided that us being friends was still incredibly important. And I couldn't have been happier. It also does what this whole book is about; it believes in me. And sure, maybe it's hyperbole to say I'd be famous one day, but the support was real and the sentiments were all authentic. She built me up. She wanted to do that. She could have torn me down and chose not to.

Jess and I would remain friends who talked on a consistent basis up until probably halfway through my time in LA. I don't know what changed, but something did. We would talk on the phone and eventually we wouldn't. I thought Jess was beautiful, she was so intelligent, and she was able to really teach me things. Most importantly, she gave me constant reminders that I was going to be okay, and that I had something special.

Jess went on to get her law degree, no surprise there. She is happily married with a daughter and lives in Kentucky. Another person who likely doesn't know how highly I regard her and how much I appreciate the fact that my life was better for having her in it. Jess, thank you for being in my corner and for saying the right things when I may not have even deserved them. I love you.

## SCRAPS

The drops of my life
Fell one by one through the strainer
Of comfort
Where I was the one caught, I was the outcast
What fell through were the pretty boys
The cheerleaders, the rich kids
The ones left behind are the ones thrown away
Pissed on and caught on fire
THE SCRAPS
My heavy fingertips escape my head
They put down what my mind converts into
Sanity
But is it?
Who am I to stereotype those fallen under the leaves
Of parental guidance
The jealous? The lucky? The envious?
As rain falls on my life like cinder blocks
On a sponge
The hardest hits
And the best mechanism for absorbing it all
They're drops of hurt, drops of tears
Drops of misfortune, discomfort, and pain
I'm here to catch them
Me
The outcast
Me
Still the person
Me
I am alive

December 28, 2002

# PAIGE

*August 13, 2004*

~Paige~

 We managed to get a lot out of the way in such a short time. I think we might even actually understand each other a little bit. There really isn't enough time and paper for me to write everything that I really feel should be written, but I will make a valiant attempt, promise.

 I do my best to never wear my feelings on my sleeve. However, often times that's where I find them, and it proved to be true when I met you. I can think myself out of any situation; unfortunately, it's not always for the best. I can convince myself that they're not worth it or that they're too good for me, or it's a waste of time when I'm leaving for college in two weeks. I want you to know though, I feel great about the recent decisions I've made.

 Plenty of times I walked through my house and said to myself "you have to stop before you get in too deep and end up screwing yourself." I owe most of it to you for being so irresistible, but I'd like to think I had something to do with my decision to allow myself to get closer. I am definitely a happier person for doing so. I don't allow myself to get too close to people because I'm a complete pessimist *and figure someone's going to end up hurt or pissed so why even start something. I'm working on allowing myself to care and feel for other people and not being so afraid to let them care and feel for me.*

*We've mentioned that as of now, this is nothing more than a good friendship, and I'm content with that. It will make both of our lives easier in the upcoming months. I'd love to come home and see you and would love to have you visit me though.*

*Those are my feelings about "us," now on to you...*

*I'm not one for significant others, or even one to try to start something of that nature. I don't get along with many people, nor do I feel many people are genuinely kind at heart. You had something different. You had an ability to pull me in and keep me always wanting to talk to you more, get to know you more, and become much closer. We only really talked on the computer until the night I went to Beechers. But that was the night that I realized you had all the makings of someone I would love to spend time with. A great personality, a passion for life, an amazing smile that could probably be seen half way across the world, eyes even brighter, and a natural beauty that isn't just stumbled upon daily. I felt I got to know you so much that night, and I loved what I got to know. I knew I definitely had a good feeling about you, and I knew we'd only grow closer.*

*You are truly an amazing person. Sometimes I get so wrapped up in you being so nice to me; I forget to tell you how highly I think of you. Unfortunately, you have the ability to sell yourself short way too quickly; you don't give yourself credit for who and what you are. That's a very talented, very fun-loving, and very attractive person. Someone deserving of probably more than I can give them, but since you've given me the chance to care about you, I'll take it. Please don't ever settle for less than what you think is perfection, because you're worth it and quite deserving of it.*

*Even though nothing can really work between us in the near future, we can always hang out when we get the chance, and there are plenty of summers ahead.*

*Thank you for being you and allowing me to be me. You are the reason age means nothing. You've shown a maturity level that would obviously attract anybody of any age. I'm just glad I got the opportunity to capitalize on what I had found. Take care of yourself and enjoy the life you have in front of you, always keeping in mind that Distance Makes the Heart Grow Fonder.*

*Love Always,*
*Jonathan Fisher*

I thought I'd lost this letter. I've written this story out before and referenced this letter, because I knew I wrote it, but just found it. Here's an essay I wrote on February 10, 2015…

*So every song on this album has a story, and there was one in particular that still takes up a huge part of my heart and holds inside of it one of the craziest stories I can tell. I was seventeen years old and her name was Paige. I've known Paige since I was about five years old and she was about three. Her brother Jake and I went to school together and became friends at a very young age. Since I was good friends with her brother, I vaguely, and through her brother, knew Paige.*

*Given our separation in school years I never really got to know Paige except always just remembering her as Jake's younger sister. As I got older and grades began blending a bit more in high school, Paige and I had come into contact a handful of times through mutual friends. She was always a cute kid and as high school came upon us she had turned into a very attractive girl, one who I wanted to get to know better.*

*To this day, many people don't understand how I tick. It's hard to explain but in one lump sum I take every chance I feel like taking and I don't think anything or anyone is off limits. If I want something, I at least make an attempt to go after it. I used to think I was going out of my league but it never stopped me. It only made me try harder and be a better me. Paige was like that for me. I honestly never really thought she'd go for me but just as my final summer before college was coming to an end, we hit it off and made a connection that was mutually engaging.*

*I sometimes look back at the me I was in high school and I can't decipher as to whether I was super cheesy or if my sincerity showed through and really made a difference. Regardless, I never let it stop me. I knew I possessed a talent that could make people smile and make them feel. I always caught flack for showing off but I can honestly tell you that I had no interest in being the center of attention, I had an interest in human interaction and experience. At that age, I don't think many others understood it.*

*At any rate, I was leaving for college and Paige was in high school. We were just finally beginning to understand our feelings, and emotions began creeping in. I did what I thought was the right thing and that was to write Paige a letter. I honestly don't remember in full what I wrote, it was eleven years ago.[8] However, I remember the last line assuring her that absence makes the heart grow fonder.*

*The day before I left for school I drove to her house in my grandfather's Buick Sable and pulled my guitar from the back seat. I remember the lengthy driveway and the adrenaline erasing the distance between my car and her front door. She knew I was coming over to see her but she had no idea I was coming in with ammunition. We went down into her basement to talk and get a chance to say*

---

8 We do now!

goodbye for the moment. If my memory serves me correctly, I gave her the letter and asked her not to read it until I left.

I was still a novice as far as guitar playing and singing went but I wanted to show her what she meant and I like being outside of my comfort zone so I wanted to play her a song. At that age, with a beautiful young girl sitting across from me, I was a bit intimidated and I remember asking her to turn completely around. Having one single person watch you sing to them is a feeling that takes some time to get used to and I had zero experience. Paige kindly and somewhat blushing turned around and I began playing. "I'd give up forever to touch you, 'cause I know that you feel me somehow. You're the closest to Heaven that I'll ever be and I don't want to go home right now."

"When everything's made to be broken, I just want you to know who I am." She turned around, beaming. What might be harder than playing for someone on an occasion such as that is the moment when they turn to face you and you kind of just look at them. I guess you hope it wasn't too awkward, that they felt the four minutes the same way you did, and ultimately that it made an impact somehow. Paige leaned in, I set the guitar aside and leaned in, and like a movie, our first kiss.

I need to explain myself in all sincerity. I didn't write Paige a letter to convince her of something. I didn't play her a song to show off my talents or to try and make her like me more. In fact, throughout my life, I have avoided relationships with people who I worried were more interested in my talents than who I really am inside. I wrote Paige that letter because I think everyone deserves the truth and everyone deserves someone taking a leap of faith for them. I played Paige that song because I thought I had a chance to give her an experience that some girls may never have. Girls deserve special treatment and to fully understand how they should be treated when someone really cares about them. I was just trying to make sure that point got across.

I think I smiled the whole way into my first day of college. I think we were both a bit naive however to think it was going to continue, but I was sure as hell willing to try. Paige was two years younger than me and in high school while I was away at college moving on to a whole new place in my life. Somehow or another, and I'll explain more later, it ended. I remember feeling a real hurt. She started dating another guy and I felt somewhat alone at a school where I knew no one.

I stayed at school the first weekend but came home the following weekend. I am a writer. I was just months removed from releasing my freshman album and was continuing to write in hopes of another. On a Friday night, I picked up my guitar and sat at the computer with one thing on my mind, Paige. I remember reading her away message (haha) about a date she was on with her new guy and I had a very simple thought in my head…you have a guy, I have a guitar, and this is war.

### THIS IS WAR

*This is war*
*And I wage it on the pretense*
*Of notions that took place*
*Long before*
*You and I could be*
*Loving this so alone*
*Living so miserably*
*You were more*
*Than just a little crush and I knew*
*You were the*

*Biggest mistake*
*I could get myself into*

*And here I Lie*
*Sleeping so silently*
*I lie awake*
*Tossing so violently*
*It's you*
*It's you I swear*

*So take one step*
*It's all I can ask of you*
*Move if you want me to*
*I'll do what you want to do*
*I could find*
*Every step that you ever made*
*Paving the way*
*And behind*
*Every last one is a smile*
*Lit so dim it disappears*
*I sing so you have to hear*
*Every song I write*

*Living so all alone*
*Grasping this microphone*
*Wishing you hadn't lived*
*Writing the worst I can*
*Pain in the other hand*
*Clenching this fist*

I was angsty as hell. I think you know this by now.

Paige and I stayed in touch a little bit but I think mostly our places in life kept us from having much of a reason. Once I was in LA, it seemed even less likely that we would stay in touch. But oddly enough, there was one single day over the course of a decade that only seems to make life feel stranger.

I had only been in LA about two months or so when I saw online that Paige was visiting family in San Diego. I really didn't know how far it was, so I didn't really bring it up. Then my dad and I walked through the door of our apartment one evening, hit the light switch, and nothing happened. Our power was out. So, I called Paige.

Armed with her uncle's directions full of "easts" and "wests," I grabbed a road map and began driving. I must have left my apartment around nine or ten at night because I remember it being late and not really arriving until about midnight at their place in San Diego. It was two friends reuniting under pretty odd circumstances. We lounged around, we kissed, we went to bed. The next morning I drove back to LA.

That's it. That was it; that's the story. But bear with me, because after that, we really didn't talk much again.

Then, the same day as the last essay, I continued telling my story. I wrote this on February 10 of 2015…

*Like I said, the engagement came to this crawl of an ending over six months. Somewhere toward the beginning of this, around February, I reached out to a friend of mine. I have no idea what made me do it but I started asking her about some of the most personal stuff that I was dealing with. It stands as one of the best decisions I've made in my life to this day. Keira was exactly what I needed during all of it.[9] She was on her own unbelievable adventure and is one of the kindest, most genuine souls I've ever had the pleasure of knowing.*

*I could sit here all day and talk about her but I need to get to brass tax. One night when I was at work, Keira stopped in to give me*

---

9  Keira is another story for another time. She was written into this essay already and I felt it appropriate to keep her in. Don't let it sidetrack you.

a bit of a pick me up. I got fudge, a journal, and a book called Love Does.[10] These kinds of actions were the kind I was used to doing, and noticeably quite uncomfortable receiving. Keira told me to write, told me to let it out, and told me to read. Adding "and who doesn't like fudge?" This book, Love Does, would eventually change my life. Not to say the book itself is completely to credit for a transformation within me, but it became the catalyst for a series of events, relationships, and ideas that created a movement of momentum that I'm still feeling. It started with Keira.

When I was at my very worst, I was reading this book and doing everything I could to try and apply it to my life. I wanted to live out loud again, be me, be inspired and inspire. I wanted to say yes, tell everyone I could that I love them and be as bold as I could stomach. It led to incredible nights with the ones I loved, early mornings and all of the warmth I could handle. I hugged more, I was more genuine and gave so much of a shit less about when bedtime was or when I had to work. Consumed with raw, unbridled passion, I needed to just be and do, because that's what love did.

One day I was at work, it was early November and I saw a post on Facebook that Paige had written. We hadn't spoken in about five years but why not, right? So I sent her a message. We talked for a quick few minutes, exchanging pleasantries and numbers and saying goodbye. However, it was a bright spot in both of our days, that part was recognizable. Simple, but I just wanted her to know I thought highly of her and so should she. That was all.

The next day, on a Thursday night, I was at an open mic and played the song This Is War by request. I played the song and as I was playing it I can remember so vividly thinking to myself, Paige has never known this song was written because of her. Not that it's

---

10   I beseech you, please find this book and read it.

very complimentary but I thought it would be funny to tell her after nine years. I texted her that night, almost embarrassed to be using her number already, but in my mind there is almost always nothing but win/win situations.

The next day we were texting a bit and she said she was sick, I remember it unbelievably vividly. I told her if she needed someone to talk to I gladly would, so we ended up texting almost all day. I had to send her the lyrics to the song and discuss it a bit, she was flattered but obviously laughing at some of the super broken-hearted teenage parts. We texted until it was time to say goodnight. It had helped me a ton to just have anyone to talk to at any time. The next morning I woke up, wished her a better day, and that was it.

Wanting to pay forward what it was that Keira and Bob Goff[11] had instilled in me, I decided I would send Paige a care package. I bought Love Does and Oh The Places You Will Go, I wrapped up a painting, a CD, the books, and a handwritten letter. I didn't have her address. I knew her former neighbor and asked if he could secretly get me her new address. The next day it was on my phone. I later came to find out that he got it by texting her and asking her for it. Coy. She later expressed how it did seem a bit odd that he would ask but she figured his parents "wanted it or something."

Five days had passed since Paige and I had spoken. I didn't really want to be a bother and sometimes need to keep my abrasive nature in check. I put the package in the mail on Thursday morning, it would be there Saturday. I would wait patiently to hear from her about the surprise, hoping she would like it. Four hours after putting the package in the mail I received a text from Paige, just checking in and seeing how I was doing. It was just one of those moments. We texted all night Thursday and I remember thinking that I wanted to

---
11  Author of *Love Does*

call her but didn't want to seem too forward. Friend or not, I know girls get hassled enough, I don't want to make things worse.

 At about eleven o'clock on November 21, 2013, Paige sent me a text asking if it was okay if she called me or if that might be weird. Of course, I was all about it. A fresh voice and point of view and all of it was so welcomed. I texted back to say that it was absolutely fine and a minute later my phone rang. We talked for four hours. It was exhilarating, it was liberating, it felt loving and honest and was never once weird. It was seamless, easy, and endless. I played her some songs and we opened up about everything we'd been going through over the last few years and how life was. She was in San Diego trying to live her dream and I was here in Pittsburgh trying to do the same.

 The conversation ended around three in the morning and I remember saying goodnight, hanging up, and quite simply just losing absolute control. I bawled, uncontrollably for at least a half hour straight. It poured out of me, it was in a way I had not cried during the entire breakup, during any break up, and almost not in my entire life as an adult. It does go to show you however, what it means to know you've survived over thinking you might not. I didn't cry this hard when my engagement ended, but I did when I knew it was behind me. That kind of emotion in overcoming the indescribable is unreal. It far surpasses the sadness, the hurt, and the heartbreak.

 I remember waking up Friday morning and writing in my bedside notebook the words "Today I woke up smiling for the first time in months." After a year of absolute agony, I was freed from the vices of thinking things would not get better, of thinking I couldn't get back what I once had and was really beginning the rest of my life. Free of anger, resentment, and unnecessary suffering. November 22 was the first day of the rest of my life, I mean that. One phone call *did that, one person, one phone number from ten exchanged lines from one Facebook post. Be bold.*

    So, there is August of 2004. There is July of 2005. Then there is November of 2013. It's this wonderfully woven story that I enjoy telling so much. It's different but hopefully recognizable. I think it does what it's supposed to do and inspires us all to take chances and do things we never thought we could do.

    After November 22, 2013, Paige and I talked constantly. It was a blast. We would talk about all of the things we wanted from life, fantasize about falling in love, and just find hope in what the other had to say. Together, we were setting our hurt aside and trying to rebuild. Knowing that this might be the simple way we could be of help to each other.

    We talked and texted all day every day. It was sort of a patch to what was ailing us but in a healthy enough way that we wouldn't destroy everything we had worked towards if somehow things didn't go well. We wanted something to look forward to. We would leave amazing voicemails for one another, early morning and late-night texts because of the time difference. It was all so much fun.

    At one point, I had the crazy idea of flying to San Diego to visit. Because this was what I was trying to reach. I wanted to stop talking myself out of things. I wanted to stop being overly cautious. What did being careful ever get me? So, I told her I thought it would be fun to throw caution to the wind, jump on a plane, and head to San Diego. On December 18, I was getting set to fly to see her. The night before I left, I sent the following email, which should give you some insight into where my head was and who I was trying to become.

Hello Dear,

    I decided that sometimes when I sit down and really just let things come out, I'm much better off. So here I am sending an email the night before my departure. It's been a theme throughout my life that my words are my greatest asset, so I'm hoping that turning to them right now is going to serve me well.

    I am simply going to try and explain myself to you in a way that is easy to understand and easily relatable. I feel like up until this point I have been completely open and honest but my message isn't being properly conveyed. So here goes...

    You already know what our first conversation meant to me. It was the culmination of months worth of misery being overcome by a new and friendly face. It was emotional. It was all part of two weeks of my life that I will always remember and that allowed me to do some soul searching. Apparently, it was exactly what I needed to experience at exactly the right time.

    My life was changing before we even had that conversation. I knew who I wanted to be and was trying incredibly hard to work towards it every day. Someone helped pick me up in one of my greatest times of need and I knew I wanted to pay that forward. I had no idea what was going to follow when I finally put that package in the mail.

    Part of the change in my life was buying into a new set of ideas. I spent so much of my relationship in a complacent state always being held back from the things I felt like I was missing out on. I used to think that's what love meant, making sacrifices and sometimes just missing out on certain things. It never bothered me as it was happening, I thought it was all for the greater good. What I realize now is that love constantly pushes us forward. It's not supposed to make us comfortable or relaxed.

*Two simple but major changes were made in my life over the past few months. The first was that saying yes was always a good idea. The second was buying into the idea that love does. I used to just think and analyze and figure out the seventeen ways everything could end. Anymore, I'm just open and along for the ride. This paragraph is what I really am always trying to put into the universe.*

*I'm not coming there to propose to you. I'm not coming there to start a relationship. I am coming there because whatever it was that we captured was undeniable and we both agreed it would have been silly not to at least see what it was like in person. I know you think that so much of what I believe has no basis in reality but who cares? Why doesn't it? Why is keeping an open mind such a bad idea even though there's the potential of hurt on the other end?*

*I have said it many times and want to reiterate that I haven't and will not have expectations. My mind has talked me out of so many things that it's time for me to take over and experience life without all the bullshit that can surround it. If I would have let my head outduel my heart, I would have never found the courage to just up and visit. I would have let it run its course and eventually we'd both lose sight of all of the incredible words we've said.*

*We've discussed so much and I think we have an oddly good understanding of each other already. I know you're going through a lot and your mind is racing at speeds so many people could not relate to. I can understand because I've been in that place and I've felt what you're feeling. I have to say once again that I am so proud of what you've already done and are continuing to do. You have yet to fail because you continue to try; it is so much more than what others have ever accomplished.*

*It seemed as though last Sunday your thoughts had finally gotten the best of you. I'm not saying that because it wasn't working in* my favor, I'm saying it because I watched it unfold. I know we both have nothing but our words to go off of but I believe we have both been very forthright and open. I think we've said things that even surprised us as they were being sent across the wire. If those words were the manifestation of our thoughts, then we are absolutely silly to write them off.

These next four days have all of the potential in the world. It is in our hands whether or not we see them through to what they can be and not allow them to fall short. Again, all I've simply asked was that we not think ourselves out of the what-could-bes and the what ifs. That we let the days come to us and keep open minds to the absolute best of our abilities. I know it's not easy and I understand that there is a giant leap of faith at stake. I myself am done with fearing. I'm not asking you to do the same, we're all different. I am just asking you to believe in this idea and in me for a handful of days.

We could be on the verge of nothing or we could be on the verge of it all. I believe we don't have time to worry which end sits somewhere in our future. Instead, we have a chance to experience life like so few allow and watch the journey fall at our feet as we try and slow it down as best as we possibly can. I can promise you I am not here for an end, I'm here for the ride. I know there are wild extremes somewhere ahead of me and also ahead of you. However, concerning ourselves with those ends will only get in the way of our nows.

I can't believe what has come of a simple response on a social media site thus far. That enough is all the inspiration I need to believe that anything is possible and that we have no choice but to embrace the opportunities we are given. I am absolutely ecstatic to see you tomorrow and to just keep these chapters rolling. I hope you will be there to embrace it all as it comes our way.

*There are so many conversations we could have if we wanted to, but let's not. We cross those bridges when we get to them. I adore you Paige. Thank you for putting light back into my life and for helping me become the person I am working so hard to become. I look forward to seeing you and your open mind tomorrow. Believe it into existence, Love Does.*

*Always,*
*Jonathan Fisher*

I showed up the next morning simply proud that I was doing this. I got off the plane, walked outside, and watched Paige pull up. After a long-awaited hug, we got into her car and headed off.

We went to breakfast at an outside bar, we went bowling, we watched TV and had snacks. We played cards and did a lot of talking and laughing. Eventually, we kissed and we fell asleep.

I was there for four days. We went to the movies; we went to dinner. We went to a party at her cousin's house. We played cards a lot, we snacked a lot, we laughed a lot. We sang karaoke, and she brought the house down. Sure, there was emotion and there were small bumps in the trip, but nothing I would ever change.

The last day we went to lunch in Pacific Beach and then we went and sat on a bench in front of the ocean. This moment was powerful. I'm sitting next to Paige, staring at the Pacific Ocean, in San Diego. Only a month removed from that first phone call. This is why we're here. This was that moment.

While sitting and talking, Paige had mentioned a certain piercing in her ear that she had always wanted. To which I quickly replied, "Let's do it, I've always wanted my nose pierced!" So, we walked a mile or so to the nearest tattoo shop, and that's precisely what we did. Together, we got the piercings we had wanted. Supporting each other, creating another memory.

We spent the rest of the evening playing cards at Starbucks until I had to head to the airport. I can barely describe the feeling of that moment. It was so simple; we weren't doing anything but spending our time together. And it was exactly what I needed. A reminder of the simple, of the easy, of taking a leap.

Paige drove me to the airport, and it was emotional. We kissed one last time, something about all of that craziness coming to an end just seemed to reach that conclusion. It wasn't easy saying goodbye, but it was easy to accept because of the decisions I had made.

That would be the last time Paige and I ever kissed. Three different moments in history, in a wonderful story. Things after that wouldn't ever really get back to being the same between us. The reality had sunk in, things got a bit weird, I sent an email that didn't land well (completely my fault), and eventually it made more sense to remove some of that passion and emotion and simply move on as friends.

Paige and I have seen each other since. She has since moved back to this area and we've gone to dinner, talked, and kept a friendship. It's been a couple of years now since we really saw much of one another, but she seems as happy as she's ever been, with a fantastic guy and a job she seems to really love. Every now and then I still see her putting some music into the world.

No matter what happens in the rest of my life, I will never forget the day that I was brought back up from the darkest place I'd ever been. How hard of a fight I had to endure, how much work I had to put in. And then, as I was getting closer, the hand that pulled me back through to the right side. I am truly, wholly, and eternally grateful.

Night three of my trip to San Diego. December of 2013. Yes, I had braces.

## YOU AND I

You and I
We have something and I know it
You know it too you just have to wait
For me to show it to you
It's proof
Like I'm a lawyer, you're the jury
And here's my biggest piece of evidence
I present to you, exhibit me
Not much to look at
Or to hear from
But if beauty is skin deep
I've got something going

You've proven to me yourself
Aspects that I've shut out of the case
Faith
Something I lack
If things should happen to go my way
I hold it off until it fails
Or falls through
And it makes me happier
To know I've once again been proven right

But you
You have a light that attracts me
And I wear black constantly
To soak in the rays
Because I don't sleep at night
And because I think too much
And because I believe in too much
I feel I've gone too far
To start heading back
So there's one place for me to go
And that's forward
Hopefully I'll see you there
Otherwise
I've been right all along

August 22, 2004

# CAITLIN

*December 8, 2004*

There's this girl I met a month or so ago at a party, her name is Caitlin. She came up to me and told me that she really loved my voice because earlier that night she had heard me playing at a party. I said thank you and was flattered by the gesture, but I couldn't get past her intoxication level. Well, this past weekend I happened to run into her again. Once again it was at a party at which I was playing. I'll never forget her sitting down right beside me the second I started and stare with an outstretched jaw; I had never felt more proud of what I had been doing. I thought this was a great thing, a few catches of course. Catches like my good friend kind of digging her or me not being a drinker, I'm pretty much lost on the situation.

It seemed like she dug me so I gave her a call. We hung out today and didn't really get close or anything but it was nice to just kick it with her around. My friend gave me the go ahead by the way. Now I'm at a stand still wondering whether it's something I should even attempt to go after due to our differences and the possibility that she wants nothing to do with me. She's got some qualities I really like; she has a great personality that compliments her ability to be herself. She's obviously a very attractive girl, but what is she looking for?

*What am I looking for? And what the hell am I supposed to expect?*

*Right now I don't know whether I call her or wait. If I should flirt with being overanxious to show interest or put the ball in her court. Not call maybe for a couple of days and see if her interest persists. She could just be looking for a friend, which is cool with me; I just can't read the situation. It's 3:30 in the morning and I have a lot on my mind, unfortunately right now it's easy to talk about this situation. I hate getting caught up in this shit because I get myself real worked up, but what is she thinking right now? Is it even at any time running through her head that she wonders what I think or how I feel? I actually kind of hope so just so I know this isn't a lost cause. Maybe I'll dream up an answer but as for now, nothing's coming out, take 'er easy.*

This is what it was like for me. All of the time. It's no wonder why I have so many different writings and why I can almost always find something to go look back on. It's fifteen years later but I still remember the kid who wrote that. He just turned eighteen, he just started college, he was a lover and emotional. He wanted to be good. He believed in love.

Here's what I find to be really wild about writing this now. When I met Caitlin, it was November of 2004. Again, I had just started college and just turned eighteen. My rough guess on when my freshman year let out is probably mid-May of 2005. That's six months. I moved to Los Angeles in the first week of June of 2005. I knew Caitlin for six months.

I think it's that six months that makes this a story to tell. It's also part of this bigger theme of partiality. Whereas, had things been given the opportunity to run their more natural course, there may not be a story to tell. This becomes more apparent to me as I dig through some of these artifacts and drudge up the memories that accompany them. Brevity, at times, creates the story.

We had this group of friends in college that still makes me so proud. It makes me genuinely emotional just to think of them and write about them now. I'll never forget the day my parents dropped me off at college, I knew nobody. I went to school by myself and wanted to let myself be thrown into the fire. As we were loading into my dorm, my dad said, "I know this sounds corny, but you're going to meet people here that will be part of the rest of your life." My Dad is like that. It's pretty awesome. And boy was he right.

What made college difficult for me at times was the simple fact that I didn't drink. It wasn't a big school, maybe three thousand kids in the entire undergrad. So, it wasn't this multitude of options on weekends. We usually went to the apartment or house of some upperclassman and partied. Again, me kind of being the guy that hung on the sidelines a bit or took a guitar, so I could stay busy and hopefully keep everyone there entertained. Often, I would take the weekends as a chance to go home and see old friends.

Once I finally became a little closer with this group, the trips home were a little more seldom, and I was finding real joy in spending my weekends at school just enjoying the time with them. The guys were great, they were a good fit. The girls were wonderful: sociable, intelligent, funny, pretty damn easy on the eyes.

I'll never forget one weekend night we all walked up to the baseball field, probably twelve of us. It was just starting to warm up and it was dark out. But it was one of the most breathtaking moments. This was my new family, my new people. This was my life. We talked, we played games, we ran around like idiots and then we laid there in the grass for hours looking up at the sky. All of us, as one.

There was a bit of dating within our group and since we were all kind of getting the lay of the land anyway, anything outside of that wasn't really common. So, I think it seemed like a natural fit for Caitlin and I to continue getting closer and see what would happen. And that's exactly what we did. We watched this amazing friendship blossom; we talked, we grew, and we went through difficulties. However, I do think we were on slightly different pages at times.

We were young, and we all had our struggles. For me, it was my first experience seeing a therapist. I had some anxiety and depression at times. I believe Caitlin had her own demons to fight, as many of us do. It's not easy to acclimate to such a change in life, we were all doing the best we could. As we grew closer, some of these demons sort of created a decision for us. I don't remember each and every memory, but for whatever reason, we never decided to actually date. But this is why I say it's the abruptness of these moments that make them stories.

It was right around this time that I also made a life-changing decision. When I look back at my life from where I am right now, that is the decision that changed every single thing that would come into and out of my life. I decided, at eighteen years old, that I was going to leave college. It was not a decision I came to lightly, nor comfortably. I didn't feel like college was exactly for me, I didn't love it the way I expected to, and I needed more out of life. So, after my freshman year, I was going to move to Los Angeles. As you know, I did.

Staying in college versus leaving presents what I think is the biggest fork in the road of my entire life to this point. Leaving those friends behind killed me. And I see them today on Facebook and the people they've become; it makes me simultaneously happy and sad. But I am who I am today because I left, and everything that my life is currently, I believe stems from that decision. I was going to go through life without a degree, wanting to be an artist, not wanting to settle, trying to do life right and by my terms.

**March 29, 2005**

Caitlin~

    The idea of this is surely new to you but if you knew me better you'd see that writing is pretty much the only way I can convey an idea. You'll also suffer the unfortunate wrath of what happens in my head when it gets late, it's now three o'clock. I will most likely sit here and write for the next few minutes and spew out things I probably didn't even know I was thinking. Many of these ideas might throw you off, many might flatter you, but they all are supposedly what I'm currently thinking.

    You might even think this is silly and laugh to all of your friends about what I did. What you do with it once it's left my hands is your business. One thing I must warn you of from my own experience, don't let my words get in the way of my ideas. All I can do is write the way I write and it's most likely going to come out poetically and easily but the bigger picture is beyond these words.

    If I'm scaring you I apologize, if your heart's racing, good. I hope that it allows you to understand how it feels to be me for only a brief moment. However, I would never wish that upon a person for an extended period of time.

    Remember that night I called you and confessed the things that were on my mind? That felt like a million bucks, but I also told you that I had written something that maybe someday you could see. This isn't one of those things I had written that day but this will give you some sort of idea as to what those things may have said.

    I can already tell this letter will be lengthy and wordy; it's just *what I'm good at. I think I write like this to delay the things I really need to say, my heart is pounding. Laugh at this if you'd like, throw it away if you'd like, keep it forever knowing someone wrote this to you if you'd like, either way, make the best of it, that's all I'm asking. I'm writing this for a reason and doing the best with what I have.*

*I guess I noticed it's Easter, which means about 4 hours ago we were talking on the phone. Perhaps it was that conversation that led to this writing, not the sole reason but gave me the drive to write something I had been wanting to write for months. Say this was an essay and I had to have a thesis statement, mine would read...*
**Caitlin ▰▰▰ and I come from opposite ends of the spectrum, but somehow and somewhere we meet in the middle; a common ground of which I never want to let go.**

*That's a start I guess because ultimately it's what I'm trying to say. We seemingly come from different worlds but for some reason we click. I don't want to know why, but it's my reality and I love dealing with it. It's when I see you, I light up. It's when you call; I get that little nervous feeling inside of me. It's when you give me a compliment; I want to keep it for the rest of my life. It's when I'm around you, I strive to impress; perfection.*

*We went on and on that night on the phone about why we would never work, etc. I understand those things, we've learned to deal with those things, but it's not always about that. It's about two people, or at least one, who feel something. It's an almost unexplainable concept, like friends in love per se. I could only find such words to explain it because I adore you. I really do. And you may never grasp my thoughts, my ideas, my being. One thing I can ask however is that you grasp yourself, and I ask to help.*

*I want to let you know Caitlin ▰▰▰ from the outside looking in. Maybe this is desperation knowing that in 2 months I will begin packing for a move that might change my life; maybe I'm digging to tell the world how I feel. To me, you've got an aura. You have a natural attraction that appeals to most everyone. Maybe you have no idea that that's the case, but I do. I can't be beside you for the next three years to tell you how amazing you are, but these few pages are my valiant attempt.*

*This is also my thank you. Thank you for giving me some sort of an interesting freshman year and letting me at least experience one college crush. I will probably tell every one of my friends this and every time I do I will probably tear up as I am now. My first ride up to Mercyhurst for orientation in September I'll never forget what my mom said.[12] "Just think Jon, you will meet some of the best friends in your life here." You know what I did? I shrugged and laughed it off. I wasn't open to that idea; I had my life and was content with it. Maybe I didn't know that people like this existed in my world.*

*You can think not so highly of my attitude and the way I am. You can construct the idea that my world is perfect and I set myself up only to scrutinize others and that I build my walls so high that nobody can get past them, it's probably true. You can also think that over your freshman year of college I played a tiny part of some guy you brushed by daily. That's fine too because like I said, it's not my life.*

*But for me, when I came home to humble Zelienople I bragged, truly I did. One of my best friends asked about you daily because it was what we often ended up talking about. It wasn't so much a dating scenario though, it was this interesting tale of opposites attracting that we always found consuming, he and I. Maybe it was because I couldn't explain you fully, or the attraction I had towards you.*

---

[12] This contradicts what I wrote before that it was my Dad who said this. I left it for a reason. The memory isn't perfect and I shouldn't expect it to be. It doesn't change the impact of the sentiment.

*I'll never forget the first day I met you, it was just funny and exciting and was my first weekend staying at school so it was a start that couldn't have been topped.*

*I never finished this. I actually just recently found it. I doubt I ever sent it.*

Once I made that decision and had those difficult discussions with my friends, it was obvious that Caitlin and I couldn't really pursue anything further. Though I believe I likely still tried, it really wasn't ever going to work. I struggled with it though, I remember that much. I remember fighting that demon and knowing that my walking away was the decision I had to live with, regardless of my feelings.

I believe I left for LA on June 6 or 7. Which means that there was a going away party for me on Sunday, June 5. The night prior, all of my college friends came together from Cleveland, Buffalo, and nearby to go to a Pirates game. I think there were twelve of us, how awesome. One of them had a connection and got us the twelve best seats in the entire place. It was a night I'll never forget. From there, the plan was to reconvene the next morning at my family's bar, since we were closed on Sundays, and have our final get together.

My friends showed up early and en masse. It was an incredible feeling. What a day. So much to celebrate, but so much sadness. It was hard to accept that it was real, or an ending, and simultaneously a beginning three thousand miles away. Friends and family were in and out all day and it felt so good to see them all coming together. The girls from college had all decided that they were going to stay at my house that night before driving out the next morning.

We had a completely empty room in our house at the time. I believe there were seven of us total, myself and six girls from school.

Which, I mean, seemed pretty damn cool. We all had sleeping bags and slumber partied on the floor. Of course, emotions running insanely high and considering how everything played out that day, Caitlin and I simply felt overwhelmed. We were inseparable for the last few hours of the night.

For the very first and what would end up being the only time in our lives, we kissed.

Lying beside one another on a night of intense highs, it was this fairytale type ending to what started so harmlessly that night on a friend's couch with a guitar in my hand. This was how it was meant to be, the collision of emotion creating this out-of-body experience. The kiss was passionate, caring, loving. It was exactly what you'd expect from two friends who had ridden the roller coaster we had been on. We knew very well that it could be the last time we would ever see one another. So, to make sure we could hold on for as long as possible, we fell asleep holding each other, taking turns crying, and wiping away tears.

The kiss made sense. It really did. There's nothing about that night that I would have changed. But it did add that bit of physicality to what had always just been emotional. And it did mess with us a bit. And this is where we as humans sometimes make our mistakes, right? We both knew what was coming, and we wanted the kiss, and were glad that we did, but we hadn't fully prepared for what was next. At eighteen years old, how could we?

I left for LA; Caitlin and I did our best to stay in touch. We emailed, we wrote letters, we talked on the phone. We were really just trying to figure out our own emotions. At some point in the future, Caitlin had even made the decision to take a small break from school to work on herself. I was in LA; it was an odd time.

*September 18, 2005*

Ms. Caitlin ▮▮▮▮▮▮▮

Well, first thing's first.[13] Happy Birthday. You have no idea how badly I wish I could be there but I am as present as possible. I really started this letter much sooner than I should have. For some reason I feel taken out of my element and I'm trying too hard to write something that will sweep you off your feet.

I hope you like everything you've gotten. Not only from me but from the others who care about you as well. Quickly, whatever you do, don't allow yourself to believe that you don't deserve everything you've gotten. I was a bit strapped for cash but I'm glad because I was more able to express myself from the heart rather than the pocket.

The song, whether you've gotten to it or not deserves a bit of an explanation. First, I apologize for it's bad quality but I only had some rinky dink recording program to record it on. I assure you I labored hard to get the best sound possible. The song is called Maps Are So Deceiving. The reason I called it that is because on paper we appear to be only inches apart but in reality it's further than I prefer to realize. I wrote it on the drive out here at a Holiday Inn in Nebraska. That's one for the Behind The Music I do!

I'm not the biggest fan of the song itself but I sent you those lyrics a few months ago and felt it necessary for you to see my expression of those words. The words are everything; it just helps to have it in a tune. Sorry for the barrage of lyrics, writing, etc. but I suppose it's what I do best.

---
13  It was only within the last couple of years that I learned that the expression is "first things first." I always thought it was meant to say first thing is first. I don't get how plural "things" are all meant to be first. Ugh.

*In case you didn't realize, which I don't expect you to, count the flowers. There are eighteen different flowers for each year of your life. The nineteenth flower is the rose. That represents you today. The you that amazes me every time I'm near. Or perhaps not even near but in thought.*

*You've been a light in my life that has been so important to me being out here. I had no idea how hard this would be, I miss you and everyone else beyond words. But just the thought of you has managed to lend a flicker of light to my every day that allows me to hang on. You never seem sad and even when I call and complain you just push me to do better, keep moving forward, and try to be happy. I couldn't ask for more from another human being. Or angel, whatever you turn out to be.*

*There are tons of things I want to say. Many I probably have before, others I may never say. Whatever the case, whatever comes out here and now, is the truth. I know at times you're probably sick of me repeating myself and telling you how great I think you are but you might only understand by spending a day in my shoes. Unfortunately, you will never get to realize how amazing you are through my eyes.*

*It's so much to realize when I think about the possibilities of seeing you. I can't grasp the idea that I will hardly ever get to see you. I guess I never realized how difficult it would be to be in the same place at the same time. The only time I've seen you in the last 3 months is somewhere in my dreams. I mean that literally, somehow you always creep in. Now I hate to say it but when you signed off on that email you sent me in June, it said something along the lines of "there is no way I wont be visiting you when you come home in July." I don't mean that in a negative way.*

*I guess what I'm trying to get at is just that idea. Just the thought of that made me smile day in and day out and I am not trying to* bring you down. Rather show you the hope you've given me. Even 'til the day you called and said you couldn't make it, I just said it's okay because at least I didn't find out any sooner and have nothing to look forward to.

I feel like there are just a million things I have left out and I'm sure someday I'll get to telling you. That or you will hear plenty of songs that may attempt to let this out. Again, I thank you for being you and for letting me be at least a tiny part of your life. However big a role I may play, I am content knowing it's what makes you happy.

They say actions speak louder than words. You see these words appear in front of you and I can only hope my actions have spoken even louder than this, however loud that may be. So again, I hope your birthday is one you will never forget and I hope somehow, in some possible way, you get everything you deserve. Because anything less than spectacular just isn't fitting. As for me, I'll try and let my actions do the talking.

I also added the live CD so you didn't have to miss the show.

*Love Always,*
*Jonathan Fisher*

Post. Script. Just one more little thing...

Erie's More Than Just a Lake, It's a Painting of a Girl.

*As I trip upon the words I write*
*To get out what I mean*
*It's hard to write so powerfully*
*To get you to believe*

*That what I say is not just words*
*Scattered on a sheet*
*But thankfulness that in my life*
*We ever got to meet*
*I remember pessimistic thinking*
*Starting off last year*
*That no one or anything special*
*Was waiting for me here*
*But as I got to warming up*
*To the idea of this new world*
*I was willing to open up my wounds*
*And see what would unfurl*
*And right before my very eyes*
*Before I had a chance*
*To see what was in front of me*
*It only took a glance*
*And there I was, hooked on her*
*Her and all her world*
*I can't believe I've lost control*
*And all because of a girl*
*Perhaps some day I'll show her*
*How lucky I now feel*
*And here I am, writing this*
*Shoulder to the wheel*
*Happy birthday beautiful*
*It's all that you deserve*
*A simple rhyme, in simple time*
*Against my every nerve.*

I have searched everywhere and cannot find the lyrics or music for "Maps Are So Deceiving." My guess is that I wrote it on paper and never saved it anywhere.

Guess what I just found two weeks later… [14]

## MAPS ARE SO DECEIVING

*These three days*
*Feel like thirty thousand miles*
*Worth of time and distance I can't erase*
*And somewhere above the New York border*
*There's a picture of your face*
*And it's taunting me*
*Asking me to come back home*
*Saying something here is waiting*
*And it might not wait too long*

*So I'm stuck here wondering*
*If every single sunny day*
*Was wasted*
*I can taste it*
*Trying to walk away*

*Is it safe to say I miss you*
*From so many miles away*
*I feel it gets stuck between Nebraska*
*And some place in PA*
*It slowly becomes a whisper*
*That can't move any more*
*And dies before it reaches you*
*Somewhere in New York*

---

[14] When I was making my album, I tried to attribute every song's title to the person for whom it was written. Because of Caitlin's initials, I had called this song 20cc. That's why I struggled to find it. Damn my creativity!

*And I'm repetitious*
*In so many ways*
*I hope you get this*
*And there's something you need to say*
*Like how you miss me*
*And maybe somewhere in PA*
*Our whispers could meet*
*And they'd have so much to say*

*Look at a map and find me*
*I'll be looking right back at you*
*It's inches on the paper*
*And that's all I have to*
*To hold on to*

A month after I sent this letter I would come back home to Pennsylvania for my birthday. I really wanted to make a trip back to school, so I planned to spend an evening there. I let a few of my friends know and chose to surprise the rest. Caitlin assured me that I could stay at her apartment. She was actually now kind of seeing someone from what I recall.

The visit was great, though somewhat odd. This was the first time we would physically see each other since the going away party. I was nervous and excited and figured I'd see where it went. When I showed up, she had made me a birthday cake. Peanut butter and chocolate; it was so good. And such a thoughtful gesture.

We all went out to some parties that evening, and I tried to make sure I visited everyone I could. Knowing I had some extra time with Caitlin, since I'd be staying there, was also comforting. But I had no idea at all what it all meant or what to expect.

We were all winding down that night and I was given a futon to sleep on. We all said our goodnights, and Caitlin was the last to leave the room and said, "I'll be back." And she was. A little while later, Caitlin came back out in her pajamas and told me to make some room. Like we'd never missed a beat, we lay there staring at one another, talking and laughing. Apparently, we eventually fell asleep.

Now, I said before that our first kiss was also our last, and that's true. The night I came back to visit, we only slept next to one another. As friends, with love. That kiss belonged where it was and neither of us seemed willing to take another shot and mess things up. This is one of the first times I remember using my emotion in a moment to decide that it's absolutely okay to have moments be exactly what they are.

Jonathan Fisher, 11/7/05

JS when I saw this card I immediately had to buy it for you, it's perfect. I know it was very different and not that easy adjusting to being in California but I hope you know I believe in you 100% and there's no one else I know that has enough heart or soul to do what you're doing. you are unbelievable Jon and you belong somewhere to showcase your amazing talent.

Your visit here was so bittersweet. I can't even tell you how wonderful it was to see you, or how awful it was to say good-bye. I hate that things are so complicated and I wish I could find the right words to say to you but someday everything will work out no matter what happens. You have a way of making me feel like nothing I have ever felt before and all I can do is thank you so much. I wish we could see eachother more often cause talking on the phone just isn't the same, being in your company is much better. :)

But hopefully we'll be able to see eachother sooner than we think. I guess we'll just have to wait and see... But I guess good things are always worth waiting for!

I appologize a million times for my lack of good time management skills cause thats why this had to come a little on the late side. Sorry :(
I hope you like the pictures I figured you'd be able to find a place to hang some of your most favorite people and things in your apartment :)

Everyone here misses you like crazy and we'd all do pretty much anything to have another private Jon Fisher concert! I miss you Jon. I hope everything is going well in Cali! Tell your brother I said hello! Dont ever doubt yourself or have second thoughts about being out there cause believe me, you were born to be a star!! Miss you!
 thinking of you always...
 Love you Jonathan David Fisher!
 ♥ Caitlin

Caitlin and I drifted after that winter. Contact was less frequent, less check-ins, life was moving on. We would reach out randomly over the years but never anything more. After graduating, Caitlin moved to North Carolina and began her life there.

In 2018, I was lucky enough to go on a small tour that took me through Charlotte. I reached out to Caitlin. She told me she would be at the show. Twelve years after the last time we had seen one another, Caitlin and I got to hug, laugh, and talk once again. It was an amazing evening, playing music for her like nothing had changed. This time as adults who understand why life is so crazy at times.

Caitlin is doing wonderfully and has met an amazing guy. She makes a difference in the world and has done such admirable things with her life. I hope we get to see one another again someday. She has pushed me to be better and inspired me to do things I may not have otherwise done. Thank you for being you and for believing in me. I love you.

2006 and 2018

### A PEACE OF MIND

I could not believe you'd say
That I should stand another day
This is where my heart's content
Where all my money has been spent
I'll just lie out on this beach
And feel the sand beneath my feet
Swim along this ocean floor
And maybe find what I've been looking for

A peace on earth
A peace of mind
A place to set my pieces
And know that I can always find

My way back to reality
Whenever I see fit
And this fist of rage stays on this page
'Til I let go of it
And maybe
Maybe next year's not so bad
I'll spend my days
In a golden haze
Shining in the sun in east LA

I can't take another day
Of the sleet and snow of north PA
Another second in this place
I wish I could say I'd like to stay
So I'm sorry now I'll just move on
And hope I'm remembered in this song
Cause each line's just my own escape
To each verse I put on this tape

And maybe this is what I need
To keep me falling to my knees
Somewhere far away and new
So I can see my world
From a different view

*January 11, 2005*

# BREONNA

WHAT I CAN TELL YOU ABOUT THIS STORY right off the bat is pretty simple. Within a couple of weeks of Breonna and I "dating," I wrote a song. It was this beautifully poetic piece about how we came to meet. "Perhaps there's a future in the dimly lit and smokey air," I wrote. "And somewhere in the days that follow suit, you'll wear the smile for me that I'll wear for you, and we'll see where it goes." The kicker was the final line, "We'd both be better off if we never met."

We'd. Both. Be. Better. Off. If. We. Never. Met. And I played it for her. I was so excited to show her what she had inspired me to create. She listened and watched excitedly as I played the song for her, then she just kind of said, "You need to change the ending." And I did change the ending, for her. Until it was over.

Breonna was my post-high school, post-college, post-LA confidence boost. After not dating for about two years, I saw her in a bar and was convinced she was out of my league. I was nineteen, she was twenty-one. She was fun, outgoing, absolutely gorgeous, and she always had a group of friends with her for a good time. I knew her sister, and I like the challenge. I sat down, we talked, I asked for her number, she gave it to me.

I tried to be super cool about the whole thing, and I waited an extra day to give her a call. I was so nervous; I had no idea what to expect. But it rang and she answered. We talked for a bit, and I asked her if she'd like to go out some time. At which point, in what would seem like odd timing, she told me that she had a boyfriend. Well, okay.

So I let it go, and I pivoted. She would still come to the bar; I'd still hang out with her. We became friends, we would hang out in a big group and just enjoy the time. Her boyfriend would come around now and again. He was a mountain of a man, as beautiful as she was, exactly what you'd expect honestly. To me, it didn't seem like the best relationship, or maybe that was my selfishly hopeful conclusion.

Our friendship continued and we became closer. We would talk on the phone, and text; we were actually friends. And if there's one thing I am good at, it's being friends with women. To the extent that I tend to put blinders up and am then blindsided when I find out they are interested in me. But if it is asked of me to be that friend, that's what I'm going to do. The phone calls got longer, the texts became more frequent. She still gave me butterflies every time I was around her, but that's part of the deal when you don't want to be an asshole.

One night, there were four of us at the bar. It was low-key. Her and I, her sister, and her sister's boyfriend (now husband). I loved this group of people, it was always such a blast, and I truly adored Breonna, so it was very easy. We were sitting at a table at the bar and playing Never Have I Ever. I really don't remember how it came to be a topic of discussion, or what exactly prompted it, but we got onto the subject of my virginity. They tip-toed around it a bit, but I'm an open book, so I had no problem letting them know that I was still a virgin. This took them by surprise.

To a certain degree, losing my virginity scared me. Mostly because I had hurt girls in the past, and I know what physicality can do to your emotions and I never wanted to be in a position where losing my virginity or taking someone else's was going to upset a break-up even further. I know that's cynical as hell, but it's where my head was.

That night we closed down the bar and went to her sister's house. It was late, everyone was exhausted, but I was in it for the long haul, always taking the moment as far as I could before knowing it had to end. Breonna's sister and her sister's boyfriend went to bed. For the first time, it was just the two of us. In a crazy series of events, we ended up having our first kiss. It was fantastic. I couldn't believe it. And she had a boyfriend.

I left the house that night around five in the morning. I had to be at work at ten for a bartending shift. But like I said, that was secondary to the moment I could have missed out on. I got up for work and she texted me. It was basically to ask that the night before stay between the two of us, which of course, I understood. This laid the foundation for what was coming next.

Within a couple of weeks we were on the phone talking and she was telling me how she was questioning being with her boyfriend, how she liked me, and so on. I talked to her about it, I tried to really be there for her, and then she said, "I'll call you back." And she did call me back, but this time when she called, she was single.

Breonna being single didn't last too long. It was more like a transition. And I was kind of amazed that this was about to happen. We had plans to hang out one night and I went to a party beforehand; I think it's all I talked about at the party. She showed up in sweats and we watched movies, and it was awesome. She was fun, she was exciting, she was different.

With Breonna, I felt so inspired. I wanted to be good for her, I wanted to show her that I appreciated more than her looks and also that good guys exist. I didn't always succeed in being as good as I could have been, but I definitely let my creativity run wild, and I think she is the reason it was so easy. For instance, look at how crazy this is. She asked me to show her some new songs some time, and here's what she got instead:

> *I told you I'd make you a CD. I only promised you one song and with all that room on a cd I didn't want to waste it. I decided I would fill er up with a few different songs that maybe you'll like. The only problem is as a musician I find all kinds of different things about songs that I like, especially lyrics. So as a writer I figured I would put on a few of my favorites and kind of add some assistance while you're listening. You may find it to be a pain in the ass. All I ask is that you don't read ahead and only read to the song you're listening to. I hope you enjoy it and find comfort in its entirety.*[15]

***1. Jack's Mannequin – Mixed Tape.***
*I figured it was the perfect way to start the CD, a song about a mixed tape. I just love the way he describes what he's doing, calls it a "symphony of sound." I never really made a "mixed tape" for someone so I figured this song explained motive. See… "it was you I was thinking of."*

***2. Carbon Leaf – Let your troubles roll by.***
*When I first heard this song I just loved the way it sounded and I liked how it kind of just put me at ease. I figured it was perfect for you in a trying time like this; it's endearing to know that someone can write something that hits home so well. I was just trying to get that theme across of "let your troubles roll by." Nobody said life*

---

[15] If you're a music nut, feel free to play along. Listen and read, there's something definitely fun about it. I created an *I Hope They're Right* playlist on Spotify.

was easy and sometimes it takes a song to help you realize. "The perfect song, at imperfect times. It's the way the chords struck with the rhymes."

### 3. Feeling Left Out – Would You Like Something to Drink?
*I actually played with these guys before, they came to my CD release in Zelie, it was amazing. They're from New Jersey and it was just a great moment so I had to put one of their songs on here. The singer is an amazing writer; he has a very poetic approach to what he says. Most of his songs are callous love songs so I put one on here that just had a nice chorus. He says "let's make the best of a great situation." It sounds backwards on paper but in theory it makes sense. Take things as they come or they might pass you by.*

### 4. Atmosphere – The Woman with the Tattooed Hands.
*I had to have one of his songs in here because after I went to his show I was just blown away by how strong the songs were. This song is so out of sorts and abstract but it's really a great story and just a perfect way of describing something he went through. "If I learned anything in my years, I've learned that I no longer believe in surprise." That's kind of a simple line but to use that so nonchalantly about such a situation is just powerful. He makes "risqué" work.*

### 5. Frank Sinatra – The way You Look Tonight.
*I don't know why this song has been like engraved in my head but it has. I just think it's an awesome throw back to a love song. He's obviously got an amazing voice and the crooner's approach to romance is just simple and perfect. There's not much more to it but it's always nice when a sentence from someone can end with "…cause I love you, and the way you look tonight."*

**6. James Taylor – Fire and Rain.**
*Just a peaceful song about a love lost. It gives hope though to the idea that what once was lost could possibly be found again. He's a great guitar player and a real songwriter. He obviously uses his music as an avenue for his feelings, I can relate. "I walked out this morning, and I wrote down this song. I just can't remember who to send it to." Nothing screams lost songwriter like a line such as that. It easily goes unnoticed but it really shouldn't.*

**7. Matt Nathenson – Suspended.**
*This song just blows me away. It was one of the first songs I wanted to put on the CD. I went to see him live a few weeks ago and as an encore, he played two songs by himself. Just he and a guitar, the last song he played was this. He sang and the crowd would follow and I could just feel the song. It's kinda the perfect love song because it doesn't do too much. He just describes this perfect time that everyone can relate to but could never put so well. "All I want to be is the minute that you hold me in. When you pretend that, I'm all that you've waited for. Time slips to nothing and I'm better than I've ever been. I'm suspended." Suspended. He couldn't use a better word to describe that feeling, it's amazing.*

**8. Jeff Buckley – Hallelujah.**
*I would assume this song has religious ties but that's not why I love it. The first time I heard it was actually on the OC and every time I listen to it, it just takes control. It's a gorgeous song the way he did it. It's a cover but the original doesn't touch this one. I just felt like a song this beautiful deserves to work its way into a lot of hearts. "Love is not a victory march, it's a cold and it's a broken hallelujah." That's rough, but sometimes reality is hard to ignore.*

### 9. The Spill Canvas – *Self Conclusion*.
*I heard this song for the first time riding in a car with a friend of mine in Cali. I think I made him repeat it until we got home. This is the first song that made me fall in love with The Spill Canvas. His approach was to write this as a playwright. He takes the words of both the man and woman and creates what he wants. He makes desperation sound enticing. It's like he's begging her to do something she wants to do anyway. She wants to pull away so bad but he knows so much what he wants that he can talk her right into his heart. "You see the trick is that you're never supposed to act on it, no matter how unbearable this misery gets." I was floored.*

### 10. Ronnie Day – *Ever and After*.
*This happens to just be a corny love song that I found on myspace but I can't stop listening to it. I love the piano part and I just think his honesty about what he feels towards the person he's writing to is noble. He separates how he feels from other guys and he's fine with admitting it, I think that's a cute expression. It's all about love with this song and it's comforting. "Our love can make disaster fade away." He's only like 17 too, which is awesome.*

### 11. Stephen Speaks – *Out of my League*.
*If someone wrote this song about me I would die. It's really one of the most amazing ways of saying something to someone. It's a barrage of kind words and I guess I can just easily relate because I often find that I'm a bit out of my league. This song helps me know I'm not alone in that feeling. "It's frightening to be swimming in this strange sea, but I'd rather be here than on land." A great analogy for how he feels. Its one of the prettiest songs I've ever heard. I would give anything to feel what he feels about the person he wrote this for.*

**12. The Scene Aesthetic – Beauty in the Breakdown.**
*Another song I found on the space. I listened to it once and played it all night until my brother got pissed. This song just screams the idea of throwing what your head says away and just going with your heart. If it's something you want, don't ruin it for yourself. It offers a kinder approach to trying to grab someone's heart. All he asks is "let's get a little closer now." All she wants is to pull away but it's about having fun and realizing you're young enough to enjoy it. You don't look for love, so why not give anything a shot.*

**13. Snow Patrol – Chasing Cars.**
*"If I lay here, if I just lay here. Will you lay with me and just forget the world?" That's true love. Sometimes when you're with someone all you want is to stop time and only bring them along. Asking that question is pretty powerful but forgetting the world is something we all need to do sometimes. Love is an easy way to let go of everything. He's asking if she would let him forget the world. It's gorgeous.*

**14. The Spill Canvas – The Night Will Go as Follows.**
*Another song where he just takes total control of the situations. In this one he's just explaining where he sees the night going in his eyes and hopes. I guess I can feel some of the words he's using like his "nervous charm." Or how he will experiment with his fears. But it always goes the way he wants and the chorus just expresses how good it's going to feel when she obliges. "...Then our lips will collide." "Forget everyone who's jaded cause they don't matter and I don't care." That carries some real clout.*

**15. The Starting Line – Piano Song.**
*These guys are more of a punk rock band but they do some great*

*acoustic songs and this piano song. I love piano in songs, especially when it's a different style from what they normally do. I just like the fact that he's convincing someone that no matter what I am going to be here and we can defy odds together. It's hard to tell if this is a love song or a song about loss. Either way all he's saying is "hold on." Sometimes those two words can be more appreciated than most people know.*

**16. Loggins and Messina – House at Pooh Corner.**
*When we were on the phone the other night I kept telling you to listen to this and I figured you didn't so I threw it on here. I think it's just a song about his son loving Winnie the Pooh and how he is seeing something like that defy generations. Either way though it's got some great ideas. I really like where it slows down towards the end. "It's hard to explain how a few precious things seem to follow throughout all our lives." He wrote a song about something like Winnie the Pooh but it's very meaningful and very pretty.*

**17. Coldplay – Fix You.**
*Obviously this is a popular song. I heard it on the radio enough times I could hate it, but I never did. I think I cried the first ten times I listened to it. It's someone trying so hard to show that they care and to show that all they want is to see you be happy. In the worst of what happens in you're life, he's saying he will be there no matter what. Add in some amazing vocals and this song will probably be a song I will love forever. Life is about hope, this song offers that. "When you get what you want but not what you need... I will try to fix you." Sometimes life doesn't make sense but we must be sure that it's going to work out. It will.*

**18. Van Morrison – Brown Eyed Girl.**
*Every time I play live I get my dad to sing this song with me. My mom's got brown eyes and I just love watching him sing this knowing after all these year's they're still in love. The song's always been fun to listen to but even better I guess when you've got a "brown eyed girl." He does and he's still so very content with that. I'm sure you can relate to what it's like being a brown eyed girl. There's no problem at all with brown eyes!*

**19. Kenny Loggins – Danny's Song.**
*As promised, here it is. I wanted to make it the last song on the CD so it wasn't so easy for you to just go right to it. I also put it here because it reflects my way of life the best of all the love songs I've heard. This song is about being real. It isn't about offering things you could never have, or talking yourself up just to get recognition, it's simply about love. He doesn't make love sound too perfect, because it's not. He makes it sound like something you can strive for but it will take work. "Even though we ain't got money, I'm so in love with you honey." It doesn't matter what you have in life, without love, it could get very lonely. There's no need for the glamour when all that really matters is that two people are in love. Someday I hope I feel so strongly about someone that the only thing that matters is the fact that I have them. That's love. That's perfection.*

*I hope you like all of these songs or at least relate to what I'm saying. I really didn't want to just hand you a CD. I wanted you to know why I put these on here and why they're meaningful to me. Hopefully when you listen to some of these they take control of you the way they did me. Music can be an amazing thing, especially the words that come along with it. Sometimes when you're trying to find* the perfect words, they're lost. Well maybe someone already said them and all you have to do is listen. That's what being lost in the moment is all about. **All you have to do is listen.**

*Always,*
*Jonathan Fisher*

Again, she really only asked for me to recommend one song. That wasn't enough for me. And I didn't think it was enough for her. When I say I become inspired, that is what happens. The connection between me and that other person becomes so intense in my mind, that I have to find ways to get it out, or I'll never sleep. I guess that's the artist part of me.

One Thanksgiving morning, I drove Breonna home, and I remember how quiet it was. I remember the billboard on the way to her house, the leaves changing colors, the serenity. But I also remember how the night before didn't go well and how everything that concerned me before was now becoming reality. That day, I wrote another song.

## SAY IT AIN'T SO

*We're beyond this*
*So called shadow of a doubt*
*We can't bear to live without these dreams*
*And the good times*
*We always brag about*
*Have seemed to fall apart at the seams*
*If we leave here*
*Content to be alone*

*Against the only person who makes us*
*Smile so wide*
*With a tear I left inside*
*That card I bought you to mistake us*

*Say it ain't so*

*We're right back here*
*Heeding none of the advice*
*We took before the fights we had*
*Or the goodbyes*
*Of a chilly autumn morn*
*Leaves painting the world drawn sad*

*I regret now*
*Saying all of the above*
*But I guess at the time I just meant it*
*I know I could have*
*Avoided every single line but*
*I knew I just had to have sent this*

*Say it ain't so*

Ultimately, Breonna and I didn't date all that long. But in that time, she did become the first person I would have sex with, and she will always be a wonderful memory. It was a crazy few months, an absolute roller coaster. It also brought out a lot in me, some negative, some positive. But I learned a lot and created a lot.

When all was said and done, I changed the lyrics back to the original from the song that I had written for her early on. I was young and angsty. Her initials were BKT, so what I once called Beautiful Kisses and Thoughtfulness, was now Beautiful Kisses and Treason. And it was no longer the ending she asked for, "To say I found the hope I thought I could live without." I went back to the original.

### BEAUTIFUL KISSES AND TREASON

*Maybe I could be*
*The reason for your sanity*
*And you could be the reason I'm still here*

*Maybe there's a place*
*Where I'm as happy as a carousel*
*I wear a smile that shines from ear to ear*

*But a place that perfect*
*Is never in the cards*
*And I'd hate to think*
*I traveled way too far*
*To end up like this*

*Perhaps we could meet*
*Somewhere in an Irish pub*
*We'll sing and dance and act like we're still young*

*Perhaps we'll find a future*
*In the dimly lit and smoky air*
*But the night still closes in and it's never won*

*And somewhere in the days*

*That follow suit*
*You'll wear the smile for me*
*That I'll wear for you*
*And we'll see where it goes*

*This is where the story starts*
*It ends where you see broken hearts*
*And shattered shards of time that we both regret*

*I'm wishing for the better*
*And I hate to write this letter*
*But we'd both be better off if we never met*

**(This is where the story starts**
**A timeline of these simple hearts**
**And shattered shards of hope from my easy doubt**
**I'm wishing for the better**
**And I had to write this letter**
**To say I found the hope I thought I could live without)**

This song went on the album Horseshoes and Hand Grenades that I released in 2008. That album was produced one year after I dated Breonna, by the guy that she broke up with me for. He and I are best friends to this day. I know for certain that I wouldn't be better off had I never met her. Most notably, because that's not how life works, and it's certainly not how we grow.

# RAE ANN

THIS IS HERE SIMPLY TO SHOW THE SONGWRITING roll that I was on at the time. This was a crush. One night we kissed. She asked me to write her a song. I wrote the song. That's basically it.

For some insider info, her initials were RAP.

**wRAPped**

Holding your hand gives me butterflies
Waiting to see if you care
If I'm grasping at something or grasping at nothing
It's me against feelings or air
And I'm holding out hope that I'm loosely
Right with direction or time
If you'll feel the same way that I felt
The same day that
I got to take your hand in mine

Or wrapping my arms around something that mattered
Wrapping my arms around hope
Wrapped up in feelings that wrapped me up
Against my will some time ago

*I promise*
*I know this isn't easy*
*I promise*
*I'm only here 'cause I care*

*And this is why I'm writing the lyrics you hear*
*And fighting these fears and*
*My mind is running away from my mouth*
*And this is the way I thought you should hear this*
*The way I felt with our first kiss*
*And I just thought that you should know*

*I'm pretty sure that you're doubting your feelings*
*Making sure all of this is real*
*But you can't hide something for the rest of your life like*
*Hiding the way that you feel*
*So I'm hoping now that you've seen me*
*Stripped down to just simple words*
*You'll stop grabbing the past and just take a leap of faith*
*'Cause at some point everyone gets hurt*

## LAST DANCE

I'll be your everything
I'll be your prince charming
I've been content with that position before
Your tone of voice oh god is so alarming
You used to say you always wanted more
From them
And now you're not with him
All you had to say was I'll never do better
Don't even try to make a lasting attempt
I should have seen that the pretty girl status
Had wrecked the way
You're ever gonna date again
It's time to bring the chorus in

Oh oh oh we've been here
Oh oh oh it's so familiar
Oh we know this is the last chance
We'll ever get to dance the last dance

All we need is a little satisfaction
A grander stage than the one we've been on
A simple task if you choose to oblige it
But if I have to ask why'd you even try it again
Let's bring the chorus back again

*I wrote this song shortly after the release of Horseshoes and Hand Grenades. I'm hoping that someday it ends up on an album. It's my dad's favorite song of mine.*

# AMANDA

Jon,
 This weekend has been absolutely perfect =] I love spending time with you and every minute spent together my feelings for you grow. I wish there wasn't so many worries and I wish I could just walk away from everything and start over with you. I'm really attempting to do that, but it's really not that easy. I'm working on it though, and I know you get sick of hearing that. But I'm for real this time and I have no more doubts about me and you. I want this to work and I don't want you to worry the last thing I want to do is hurt you. I'm sorry I'm not good at expressing my feelings and I'm not good at talking about stuff. I never have been I guess I just deal with stuff differently, but I can type it =] when I'm with you all I can do is smile. When we're not together all I do is think about you, not having a worry in my mind because I know that you are doing the exact same thing. That really means so much to me. Thank you so much sweetheart

Love always,
Amanda

Jon,
I really have no idea where to start. I guess by thanking you for being so patient with me and by not giving up. That really means alot to me & shows me how much you actually care. After talking to you last night made me realise that I could have everything I wanted & be happy by just looking at what's in front of me. I don't care about the flowers or whether or not we go to fancy dinners. I would rather know you think about me. to know that you are happy thats all I really look for in a relationship. I think we can potentually have a strong relationship. Anyone else would have given up by now, that is so sweet. I feel horrible for being so stubborn but through all this I've lost one but gained so much more. I know what I need to do and I'm going to attempt this once again. everyone has made me see that I have friends who care & one amazing guy willing to help me through it all. I woke up this morning & cried while I got ready for school b/c Josh never called me back last night & I was proved wrong. I'm so sick of trying to defend Josh & I'm sick of making up excuses for

him so I can sleep at night. I can't ask for much, but it says a lot when I can't even get a simple text or a phonecall out of him so therefore we decided its not worth giving up someone who does all that stuff & I don't even have to ask ☺ you really are one of a kind ♥ & I think we could work. It says a lot that I can't find 1 bad thing about you & I could go on & on with things I love. from the way you look at me, to the letters I keep in my purse & I love how you find my odd eating habits cute. I love everything about you b/c it makes me happy ☺ & I even love it when we argue b/c I can't stay mad at you & it makes you that much more irresistable ☺ but I want it to work. I really do want whats better & I'd be stupid to ~~throw~~ say kno. you amazing & wow. just wow. ☺

♡ Always,

Amanda

*im sorry it rambles on & doesnt make much sense ☺ my hand hurts tho*

As you can see, I did try very hard. I had an unwillingness to accept failure at times.

Something about the timing of dating Amanda brought the absolute worst out of me. I was not in a good place. We barely dated, but I handled it horribly. One night, she called to tell me that she didn't think it was going to work. I hung up the phone, I walked to my door, and I punched three direct holes straight through it. The biggest problem with that kind of rage is an inability to understand pain in real time. What I would later realize is that every time my hand had pulled back through the door, my arm was catching the brunt of it as the wood tore through me.

I walked out of my house and down the street. I called my friend and vented. My arm was in terrible shape; my mind was a mess. I don't know how common it is for this kind of anger to take someone over, but I did deal with these issues at times growing up. Worse than any of it was the next morning, when I woke up, and realized the only thing I had accomplished was having to buy a new door.

I've come a long way since the times when anger controlled me. When I couldn't slow myself down for the brief moment it took to make a better decision. I'm proud to be far removed from those feelings and that loss of control. However, it did eventually create a song that made its way onto the album. I'll let the lyrics speak for themselves.

### PERFECTION

*I know you're scared well I'm scared too*
*I only wanted to be with you*
*And I'm sorry everything I said I meant*
*I'm sure I scared you*

*They've said I'm way too cocky
But that's just the way it's got to be
Because why not feel that way
If you're me*

*I write the perfect songs at the perfect times
I've written chords upon chords to the perfect rhymes
And I don't have to stop after I write each line
It's perfection each time*

*I found that knife wound where you stabbed me
In the back what a thing to see
Bleeding on that rug you always hated
Did you know that perfection bled green?*

*And right along with it came these lyrics
So I figured I'd write them out for all to see
I just had to find the chords
That summed up me*

*The problem is I'm incapable of flaw
And I'm sure that's jealousy that I just saw
And I can't wait to hear this song's applause 'cause I'm perfect
And everything else is just because*

# ELYSE

THIS IS ACTUALLY A VERY LATE ADDITION TO THIS BOOK. As I read through my drafts, I felt like there was an abrupt ending with the Amanda chapter. I alluded to this relationship earlier, and this isn't the place or time to get into the details, but to wrap things up on that part of my life, I'll explain slightly.

After all of that dating and the craziness of the years after I moved home from LA, I did eventually find someone to settle down with. Elyse and I knew one another from high school, and we actually kissed once my senior year. In the magnitude of our relationship, I think that's a hilarious anecdote. On December 23 of 2007, Elyse and I began our relationship.

This is a pretty obvious reason for the stories to have stopped. It was a natural place to begin the rest of my life. Very early on, I did write a song for Elyse.

**TWENTY-ONE**

*Sometimes these words fall off my tongue*
*Sometimes I'm twenty-one and wishing I was young*
*And it'd be great to fall in love*
*But it's always easier said than done*

*If I watched you break your heart*
*I'd pick the pieces up and let mine fall apart*
*And I'm not saying this to brag*
*But to mend a broken heart I'd write a song in seconds flat*

*Just believe in me*
*You'll see things you've never seen*
*You may never see again*

This is another song that I hope to put on an album someday. I also hope that I get the opportunity to tell this story in its entirety and to explain the way my life changed after it ended. Elyse and I would go on to spend about five and a half years together. Though it didn't end the way we expected, it did end the way it was supposed to.

I'll always be grateful for what it taught me and for the strength that I gained from it. The rest of my life was just beginning, and I barely knew it.

# SUMMATION

**AS I BEGAN RIFLING THROUGH FILES TO SEE WHAT ALL** I had, my discoveries amazed me. Though not all up to my standards, I've uncovered over three hundred and fifty pieces of work. Poems, lyrics, essays, letters, and even some books I had started and never finished. Some of these works you have seen in this book, others I couldn't find a spot for, or they were awful.

These pieces of work and the characters in this book are who I am. I'm emotional, and I'm sentimental. At times, I'm angry. I try to find a way to live life that not only inspires me, but will also inspire others. A life in which I take chances, and fight for what I want. I look at vulnerability as one of the greatest strengths a person can possess.

I hope the characters in this book will one day agree that I have done our stories justice. That they match my fondness for these memories, and regardless of where we find ourselves in life, reminiscing about these days will still bring a smile to their faces.

As I was writing this book, a friend asked me, "Why did you keep all of this stuff for so long? I'm sure there were times when you felt like it should just be thrown away." I knew the answer to this question because I've asked myself the same thing. Many people have had these same notes, these same conversations, all of it.

Eventually, they get lost in a move or dumped for space and a fresh start. But I believe there is no reason to have regret, and I always want my past to help shape my future.

To answer the question of why I kept it all, here's what I can say: Personal connections mean everything to me. Even if they're momentary, they can be impactful. People deserve to be treated with the utmost dignity and respect. This book is my way of paying tribute to that ideal.

When someone handed me a note in school, I didn't read it and toss it. I took it home, and I put it in a box. The same with a letter, a picture, or anything else that seemed genuine. Because I wanted to dignify that person's efforts. I wanted to be sure that they weren't discarded as though they meant nothing to me, because as you can see, their efforts meant everything to me. The fact that someone took time to write me a note, to mail me a letter, to put thought into something they wanted to say and have me hear; it astonishes me. It makes me feel like I'm the luckiest guy on earth.

No one owes us their time. No one owes us their feelings. But eventually, I do think we connect enough to want to share those things. And look at these connections. Twenty years later, I am writing about them and the impact they not only had on me then, but have on me today. They believed in me, and honestly, I think they still do. I don't take that lightly. I needed them; they were instrumental in my growth. I won't soon forget that.

This book is about honoring the people who took the time to build me up. Who took the time to really become a friend. And I know I didn't tell every story, and there are characters who are left out. This doesn't minimize their impact, I promise. I just think there's a time and a place. I hope that there is a future for us to share in those stories as well.

Life is beautiful. It's tragic and full of pain and heartbreak and intense heartache. But it also gives us the most profound moments if we choose to embrace them. It gives us memories, it gives us triumphs, it gives us human connection to such a degree that we often fail to completely understand it. If we allow ourselves to live inside a moment, in real time and without the distraction of what ifs, we can turn five hours into a lifetime. We can simply be, nothing more.

My hope for you, as the reader, is that you found inspiration here. I hope you laughed at my shamelessness, and I hope you accepted my vulnerability. I hope you experienced emotion right along with me. I hope you've been inspired to access those old memories. Or to find some old pictures or notes. That you are reminded of the beauty of life and the daily decision we get to make to truly live.

# EPILOGUE

I'm writing this as I'm about seventy-five percent done with the initial draft of this book. It seems like an odd time to write my epilogue but earlier today, in a stack of notes I had missed, I found this.

> Dear Jon,                              May 17, 2001
>
>     Hey hun, I was reading my yearbook from last year and I was read what you wrote to me. I was reminded of all the times we have shared... some of them I almost forgot about. But I just felt the need to write you a letter about how much you mean to me and how much you have saved me these past few years.
>
>     We started out our friendship kind of in a weird way, a relationship, BUT this is the best friendship that I have ever had with a guy before. I feel like I can share anything with you, tell you my secrets and trust you not to tell anyone in return. We went through a lot in the years but we proved not only to everyone else but also to ourselves that we have a true friendship and it is something that can never be broken. I'll never forget the football game that I started liking you at in 8th grade. I had the world's biggest crush on you. I thought you were the cutest, most adorable guy in the world. (I still do)... But from that point on we had a rough relationship, always going out and breaking up. BUT we didn't let this stop us from being friends. In fact, I think it actually brought us closer to one another. I have so many conversations saved with you and so many memories with you that I will NEVER forget. Homecoming was perfect all because of you! And then just a few months ago when we watched movies at your house and we kissed... those were times that as long as I am alive I will remember, because they are SO SPECIAL to me! I think a lot about what we would be like if we would have ended up having a long term relationship one of those times, and I still don't know what it would be like. But that is something that I will never know but what I do know is that we have something that very few people have. And that is the best friendship someone could ask for. There are times when I could sit with you and talk for hours about anything and everything and know that you understand every single word that comes out of my mouth. There are 3 people in this world that know my moods, Mandy, Tabitha, and YOU! And believe me I am a really hard person to understand. But you still know everything. I feel so comfortable around you, I can always be myself and know that you will love me for me, not for someone I am not and I thank you from the bottom of my heart.
>
>     Okay...now the really hard part... When I think about everything you have said to me to make me feel happy, and how you have supported me, there are a lot of different

memories that come to my head just because you always do support me. But the one time that I will never forget is this one...I never told you this but I want you to know...Here goes...well a while back this school year, I got in a fight with my 3 best friends on a ski trip, Tabitha, Liz, and Maggie. I think you remember, but if you don't this was when I liked you a lot and we were kind of on the verge of going out. Well I was so incredibly upset about this, that I didn't know what to do. I came home that night a wreck and I was in my room crying I thought about killing myself. I was on the verge of doing something so stupid that wouldn't have solved anything but I felt like it was all I had. But then I looked up at my wall and there was your picture. It was a picture of you and me at homecoming and then your presents you bought for me for Valentine's Day and some poems you had wrote to me. Well as I looked up I remembered that you were there for me and that I wasn't alone, that night I saw you and you saved me. I don't even want to think about what would have happened if I wouldn't have looked up but all I know is that God made me look up at you and feel your love, because at that moment, I didn't feel alone. You saved me Jon, and I can't thank you enough for it. No one knows this story but you and I trust you not to talk about it because it's personal. But I thought you should know how you saved me.

    So basically Jon, this letter is a thank you for everything you have taught me and done for me. You don't know what you mean to me and I think that as long as we live, we will always be close. I love you and there is nothing else to say but thank you from the bottom of my heart!

Love Always and Forever,<br>Dana*

*Jon-here are some things I found on my computer from you and I thought they would be good to give to you, even though most of it you have already seen...*

You treated me like I was your princess and you were my prince
You felt something that my heart simply missed
I'm Sorry,
For all those times I just said no
For all the love I would never show
I'm Sorry,
For all the times I made you cry
For all the times I would never try
I'm sorry,
For all the times that I messed up
For all the times I gave our love up
I'm sorry for hurting you
I never realized our love was true
Until I lost you...

dA▇▇▇24: ok I have an idea...lets make a pact
J Dawg Fish: Hehe, okay:-)
dA▇▇▇24: lets promise each other to call each other and talk on here and be like Best friends to each other and not let a good friendship fade just bc we dont have a thing and lets try to hang out more
J Dawg Fish: Definitely
dA▇▇▇24: promise?
J Dawg Fish: Promise

"A real friend is one who walks in when the rest of the world walks out."

Open the window
Let the sunset in
If only for the last time
Let me see you smile again

I'll take my records
You can have your books
I'm sorry I never read them
But, it says so much about us

Always trying
To make love out of care
The perfect recipe
But, something wasn't there

Chorus:
And I wish you
Sunrays and Saturdays
Perfect starry nights
Sweet dreams and moonbeams
And a love that's warm and bright

Sunrays and Saturdays
Friendship strong and true
Oceans of blue and a room with a view
To live the life you choose

You'll write me letters
And I'll call you on the phone
A wire away from touching
And never quite alone

We'll get to know ourselves again
And we'll heal our hearts
It's not that we're bad together
We're just better off apart

Always trying
To have one and one make two
And even though it never worked
I still feel love for you

Chorus

> Have you ever wanted to love someone with everything you had, but that other person was too afraid to let you? Too many of us stay walled because we are too afraid to care too much ... for fear that the other person does not care as much, or at all. Have you ever loved someone and they had absolutely no idea whatsoever? Or fell for your best-friend in the entire world, and then sat around and watched him/her fall for someone else? Have you ever denied your feelings for someone because your fear of rejection was too hard to handle? We tell lies when we are afraid...afraid of what we don't know, afraid of what others will think, afraid of what will be found out about us. But every time we tell a lie the thing we fear grows stronger. Life is all about risks and it requires you to jump. Don't be a person who has to look back and wonder what they would have, or could have had. No one waits forever ...
>
> *Well those are just some of the things that remind me of you and thank you again...I love you!*

One of the first things I wrote for this book was the prologue, because I felt like it gave me a path to follow. It created my mission. I had no idea where the book would take me, and I hadn't even unearthed all of the things you've gotten to see and experience. I knew that I was inspired by my past and those in it, to create something beautiful. Not only for me, but for them. And for you.

I wanted to share these stories because they're personal and because I could. Truthfully, to this point, I've written about one hundred and fifty pages frantically over the course of seven days. I've mostly felt like my stomach was being ripped out. My friends told me to stop before I drove myself insane. My process seemed to be too intense, like this might be a path to destruction, drumming up all of this old emotion. It's been difficult. I've had trouble sleeping. But this is my dream, and I do believe we suffer for our art.

By now, you're aware of why I titled this book *I Hope They're Right*. And when it started, I wanted to give myself the reminder of what I was doing. **But at times, it is hard to be convinced that I can do something that changes the world.** What I truly never saw coming was this ending, and knowing that I already have.

Do good today. Do good every day. Expect nothing in return. I love you.

## ABOUT THE AUTHOR

Jonathan Fisher is a first-time author with *I Hope They're Right*. He started writing as early as eight years old and has written since. This book is the product of that work and passion, and he hopes there is more to come. Jonathan is a volunteer big brother through the Big Brothers Big Sisters program and enjoys giving back when possible. Jonathan resides in the Pittsburgh suburbs with his Himalayan, Lyle, and his dog, Chief.

Made in the USA
Middletown, DE
17 December 2021